To Jo—

Best wishes

Robert Lee

Granddaddy

The front cover photograph is of James Erskine receiving the
Military Cross on behalf of his son Tommy from King George V
at Ibrox Park football stadium.

Granddaddy

ROBERT LEE

Matador
9 Priory Business Park,
Wistow Road, Kibworth Beauchamp,
Leicestershire. LE8 0RX
Tel: 0116 279 2299
Email: books@troubador.co.uk
Web: www.troubador.co.uk/matador
Twitter: @matadorbooks

ISBN 978 1800461 826

British Library Cataloguing in Publication Data.
A catalogue record for this book is available from the British Library.

Printed and bound in the UK by TJ Books Limited, Padstow, Cornwall
Typeset in 11pt Minion Pro by Troubador Publishing Ltd, Leicester, UK

Matador is an imprint of Troubador Publishing Ltd

This book is dedicated to the memory of Tommy, Ralph and Barrie Erskine, and of Jack and Bert Lee, and all the other brave men and women who gave their lives in the two world wars.

Author's Note

Much of the content of this book comprises diary entries and excerpts from letters. In general they appear as they were written, with only occasional alterations for clarity, and cuts are indicated by … (An exception to this had to be made for my grandfather's letters – had I published in full his declarations of love for my grandmother, this book would have been twice as long.) The writers have inevitably saved time (and paper) by the liberal use of abbreviations. Where these occur I have, for ease of understanding, used the appropriate full word. As it's easier on the eye, I have also used the contemporary convention when recording dates and times – eg 21 June not 21st June, 4 pm not 4 p.m.

Many of the places referred to in Flanders are now known by their Flemish name rather than their French one – eg Ypres is now Ieper, La Clytte is De Klijte. I have stuck to the original French names which were in use at the time.

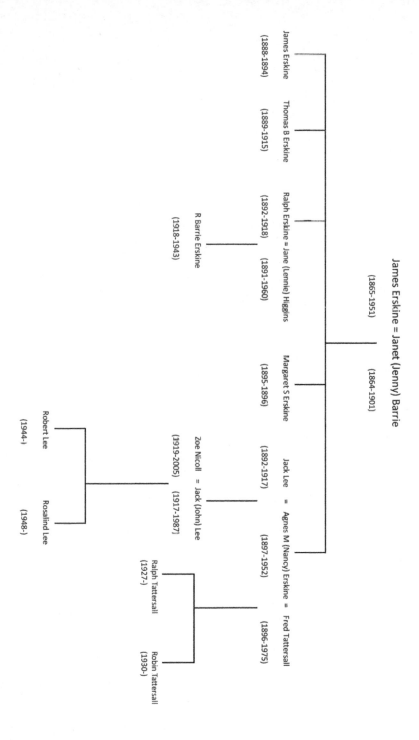

JAMES ERSKINE FAMILY TREE

James Erskine = Janet (Jenny) Barrie
(1865-1951)   (1864-1901)

James Erskine (1888-1894)

Thomas B Erskine (1889-1915)

Ralph Erskine = Jane (Lennie) Higgins
(1892-1918)   (1891-1960)

R Barrie Erskine (1918-1943)

Margaret S Erskine (1895-1896)

Jack Lee = Agnes M (Nancy) Erskine = Fred Tattersall
(1892-1917)   (1897-1952)   (1896-1975)

Zoe Nicoll = Jack (John) Lee
(1919-2005)   (1917-1987)

Robert Lee (1944-)

Rosalind Lee (1948-)

Ralph Tattersall (1927-)

Robin Tattersall (1930-)

CONTENTS

FOREWORD

In October 1948, when I was aged four, my father, who worked for ICI, was promoted to a position as a sales manager in Blackley, North Manchester, and my family relocated from London to Timperley in Cheshire. This involved an all-day journey I can just remember, crammed into an Austin 8 a decade before the M1 was built.

My mother was heavily pregnant at the time and gave birth to my sister Rosalind two months later. In those months, and quite often thereafter, I was looked after at the house of my paternal grandmother Nancy, known to me as 'Nan', who lived in nearby Didsbury with her second husband Fred Tattersall. The third member of the household was a kindly, white-haired old man whom I knew as 'Granddaddy'. He was Nancy's father James Erskine, my great-grandfather.

Granddaddy was a short compact man, barely five feet six inches tall, with keen humorous blue eyes, a vigorous growth of short snowy white hair brushed upwards, and a bushy regimental-style moustache. He was softly spoken with what I now know is a Scottish accent and he always took a great interest in me. Erskine is my middle name and Granddaddy was very proud of this. He used to say 'I am James Erskine of Scotland and you are Robert Erskine of England.' We used to play games together a lot. He taught me dominoes and draughts and was hugely encouraging when I started to learn to count and read. Most of my memories of him are from photographs but one small incident still sticks in my mind. I was spending the afternoon there because my mother was taking her driving test. When she returned, I rushed over to tell her that I had won at dominoes. Granddaddy gently admonished me, saying 'You're not the only pebble on the beach' and going on to explain what that saying meant – my mother had passed her driving test. To this day I think of him whenever I hear that expression.

I only knew him for a short time as he died three years later, but from what my parents told me, he had been an interesting character; a Glaswegian who held and promoted strong left-wing views, with a passion for athletics and horse racing. He suffered the tragedy of losing his two sons in the Great War, and was so traumatised and disillusioned that he spent the next 25 years as a virtual hermit, living in a cottage on a hill outside Glasgow.

My father died over thirty years ago, and left a veritable trunk-load of letters and memorabilia. More recently, after I stepped down from the rat race of corporate life, I undertook the Herculean task of going through these and digitalising some of them. With the help of genealogical websites, and the National Archives at Kew, I have managed to piece together a more complete picture of Granddaddy's life. I was also lucky enough to be able to draw on the memories of his grandsons, my uncles Ralph and Robin Tattersall.

Here it is – the story of James Erskine of Scotland – Granddaddy.

Acknowledgements

In compiling this book, I owe my gratitude to several people.

Special thanks to my uncles Ralph and Robin Tattersall for sharing their memories of Granddaddy. I've drawn extensively on Ralph's recollections, both written and oral.

To John Hartley for his permission to quote from his excellent history '6th Battalion The Cheshire Regiment in the Great War.'

To Therese Tobin for her professional advice, for teaching me to punctuate, and for putting so much effort into proof-reading.

And to my sister Rosalind White, and my cousins Rosaleen Lee and Caroline and Sue Tattersall for their unfailing encouragement and helpful suggestions.

1

A JOURNEY TO THE NEW WORLD

By the middle of the 19th century the industrial revolution had propelled Glasgow from a small mercantile town into a thriving industrial city, the powerhouse of Scotland and the second largest city in Britain. Powered by the Lanarkshire coal field and by nearby iron deposits, and with the river Clyde as an outlet for exports, there was a massive boom in heavy engineering, including shipbuilding as well as the traditional textile manufacturing. With this explosive growth inevitably came over-crowding, poverty and ill health.

Granddaddy's father, also named James Erskine, was born in 1823 in the notoriously poor Gorbals district, the eldest of four children of William Erskine, a house painter, and his wife Agnes. James worked in the textile industry and is variously described as a pattern setter and a Jacquard cutter. A Jacquard machine, named after its French inventor, made use of a series of punched cards joined together in a continuous chain on which a fabric design was stored. Life for James would have been pretty grim and, like many of his compatriots at that time, he made a brave decision to seek his fortune in the New World.

Shortly after his 26th birthday, James set sail in a ship called the *Malabue* from the Glasgow port of Greenock, and on 31 May 1849 he arrived at New York, after what would then have been a pretty uncomfortable voyage. From there he travelled about 200 miles north-west to the small town of Clinton in Massachusetts. Clinton had established a textile industry and was a pioneer in the development of Jacquard machines and he found employment there. He must have made a success of it because a year later he was joined by a young lady from Paisley called Margaret Jamieson, who arrived at Boston on 21 May 1850 on the SS *Lady of the Lake*. Presumably she was a long-standing girlfriend as a week later, on 28 May, James and Margaret were married in the Clinton Baptist Church.

The next year they had a son, William Erskine, born on 20 February 1851. However, the following year tragedy struck the Erskine family when young William died aged 19 months. Cause of death was recorded as 'inflammation of the brain': meningitis, presumably. The following year they had a daughter who they named Margaret after her mother.

For what reason we shall never know, James and his family returned to Scotland, where in 1855 they had a second daughter, Agnes. But two months later, they had a second infant death – young Margaret succumbed to scarlet fever aged two. The Erskines then headed south to another large textile centre, Manchester, where a son John was born. By 1861 they had returned to Glasgow, where they had another daughter. Somewhat bizarrely, they also named her Margaret. Even more bizarrely, and sadly, this Margaret too died three years later, also of scarlet fever. By this time the Erskines had lost three children out of five — a low survival rate even for Victorian times.

The following year, in 1865, they had their final child, another son, my great-grandfather. Undeterred by their previous experiences of naming an offspring after its parent, they named the boy James. And he was destined to live an eventful life, and to raise an amazing family.

2

JAMES ERSKINE
– EARLY YEARS,
MARRIAGE AND FAMILY

James Erskine – 'Granddaddy' – was born at 8.45 am on 8 October 1865 at 16 Lady Lane, Paisley. When he was small, the family moved to the more upmarket 30 Portland Street in Glasgow and James overcame any problems with his social background by gaining a place at the prestigious Allan Glen's Academy. By the time of the 1881 census the family had relocated north of the river Clyde to Great Eastern Street in the Parkhead district, and the 16-year-old James had a job as a stockbroker's clerk. By now his sister Agnes had married a draper's clerk, William McDonald, and his older brother John was working as a commercial traveller for a stationery company.

Four years later, when James was 20, his father died of heart disease. Two years after that, James got married. His bride was a shop girl whose full name was Janet Penman Barrie, though she was always known as Jenny. Jenny was the fourth of eleven children of Thomas Barrie and his wife Margaret.

Thomas Barrie was a blacksmith who worked in the huge Parkhead Forge. This had been established to make forgings and iron plates to supply the burgeoning Clyde shipbuilding industry. By the late nineteenth century, it had grown to the largest forge in Scotland, covering 25 acres, and specialising in armaments and armour plate for warships. It finally closed in 1976 and the site is now occupied by the large Forge Retail Park.

Thomas clearly excelled at his profession and eventually became a forgemaster. He made a good enough living to purchase some properties in Salamanca Street, in the Tollcross district. These produced an income for his heirs until as recently as the 1960s, when they were sold, fetching only a few hundred pounds. However, he didn't live long enough to retire and enjoy the fruits of his relative wealth. On 3 September 1890 he went missing, and three days later his body was found in the River Clyde, near where the Erskine Bridge now crosses it. There was what appears to have been a fairly perfunctory inquest and a verdict of suicide was returned. This was perhaps a convenient conclusion – the anecdotal evidence passed down gives a more plausible explanation, simply that Thomas had fallen in after consuming a few bevvies too many. He was only 52.

Thus Margaret was widowed at the age of 50, having borne Thomas eleven children in 23 years. Whether she held these views before this incident we don't know, but she became a strong advocate of the temperance movement, which she supported in Glasgow for another 27 years until her death in 1917, when she was given a public funeral by the Salvation Army.

The Barrie family lived at 78 Gray Street, a relatively prosperous road near Kelvin Park, and after they were married, James and Jenny moved into the nearby number 96.

The year after their wedding James and Jenny Erskine had their first child, who they also named James. Had he been American, he would have been James Erskine III. A second son,

Thomas Barrie Erskine, followed in 1889 and, after a four-year gap, a third son, Ralph.

Then the first tragedy struck James and Jenny. A few days before his sixth birthday, little James died after suffering from pneumonia and peritonitis.

Infant mortality was of course not rare in those days, and a year later another child came along, this time a daughter, Margaret Strachan Erskine. (Margaret Strachan was Jenny's mother's name before her marriage.) But fate had another blow for the Erskines when little Margaret also became an infant death statistic, fatally catching tubercular meningitis at the age of only eighteen months.

James and Jenny had lost two children out of four, well above the average mortality rate at the time. But Jenny was still in her thirties and they were able to have a fifth child. This was another daughter, christened Agnes Muriel Erskine, but always known as Nancy, born on 7 September 1897. Nancy was my grandmother.

So as the twentieth century dawned, James and Jenny had lost two of their five children but they at least had two healthy sons and a healthy daughter. But in 1901, James was to suffer an even more grievous blow. Jenny contracted tuberculosis, or 'consumption' as it was then more commonly called, from which she tragically died at the age of only 36.

Thus Granddaddy in his mid-thirties suddenly found himself a widower, with three children aged 11, 7 and only 3. He had worked at various jobs, including being a fruiterer, and now earned his living selling insurance. Not unreasonably, he decided that he couldn't manage all three children as well as his job. Initially the young Nancy moved in with James's older sister Agnes and her husband William McDonald, a bookkeeper, who lived in nearby Dennistoun. But that arrangement was not to last because, only three months after Jenny's death, Agnes too passed away at the age of only 45.

Care of Nancy was then undertaken by Jenny Barrie's younger sister Margaret, who was four years younger than Jenny, and her husband John Black, a civil engineer. As a professional man, John will have earned a good salary, and his job had previously taken him to work for the American Bridge Company in Philadelphia. The Blacks had no children of their own and they cheerfully took on the task of raising young Nancy, while James concentrated on bringing up his boys Tommy and Ralph. Initially the Blacks lived in Kidderminster, but then John's work took him to Matlock, where Nancy went to primary school, then to Aberdare. There Nancy went to Aberdare High School, where she had a glowing academic record.

Unsurprisingly given his childhood experiences among some of the worst living conditions in Britain, James was well aware of the need for social change from the injustices and despair of the times and he became immersed in left-wing politics. (My mother told me that he was the campaign manager for James Kier Hardie, the trade unionist and founder of the Scottish Labour Party. But I've not been able to confirm this or indeed to identify which campaign it might have been. Kier Hardie did make a speech at Nancy's school in Aberdare, though.)

James was also passionate about education, and determined that his children should have better opportunities than he had had. The boys were bright and won bursaries to follow in their father's footsteps to Allan Glen's School.

Granddaddy's other passion was athletics. Always supremely fit, he took an early interest in the athletics scene, especially cross-country running. In 1885 he was a founder member of the Clydesdale Harriers Club, and subsequently served as its secretary for many years. Running through the streets of Glasgow in shorts, almost a century before 'jogging' became fashionable, he must have raised many an eyebrow.

3

WORLD BOXING
CHAMPION

T ommy and Ralph each became excellent athletes and both were heavily involved in sport at Allan Glen's and subsequently Glasgow University.

One of James' nephews, George Barrie, was a champion middleweight, and one evening James and the boys attended one of his fights. After the fight, George invited anyone in the crowd to go in the ring and spar with him. Ralph Erskine, aged 16, volunteered and George was so impressed with his natural ability that he persuaded Ralph to enter the regional championships. This he did, and duly won the featherweight division, before going on to win the Scottish title in Edinburgh.

The next few months of Ralph's career were summarised by an article written in the Glasgow Herald in 1938.

His career was probably the shortest and most sensational on record. It extended from start to finish for about six months, during the whole of which time he was a 17-year-old Allan Glen's schoolboy. In the course of these six months he won a Scottish National open tournament, the Western District and Scottish Championships, The English Public Schools Championships, and the European Championship, at the National Sporting Club in Paris.

In the Amateur Boxing Association Championships at the Alexandra Palace he was adjudged the loser on points in the final bout after boxing at intervals all day from 10 am till midnight, each bout consisting of two three-minute rounds and one of four minutes. His opponent was a man who had already won during that season 16 open competitions.

The 'Sporting Life', the 'Sportsman', the 'Times' and 'Boxing' agreed that Ralph Erskine should have been declared the winner*. The 'Life' went out of its way to say that he was 'the most desirable type of amateur that had ever competed in these championships' notwithstanding the fact that Oxford and Cambridge men were frequently competitors.

'The Times' expert wrote that 'not only was he beautifully trained, but he must have been taught by a past-master in the art of boxing.' As a matter of fact he had never received a professional boxing lesson in his life nor seen a boxing bout or a boxing ring until he climbed over the ropes for his first tournament at the National Sporting Club, neither had he been 'trained' in the technical sense.

In those days it was firmly believed in Scotland that the only way to get a decision over an English boxer was to knock him out!

Despite this controversial defeat, shortly afterwards Ralph was chosen to represent Great Britain against America and, in May 1911, he was in a party of boxers who sailed to New York on the SS *St Louis* to take part in a tournament. The other boxers in the team were a mixed bunch:

Frank Parks, heavyweight, from Kings Cross, aged 36, who had been ABA Champion in 1899 and 1901/2/5/6. He became well known in the business and masonic world before he died in a car accident in 1945.

Reuben Charles Warnes, middleweight, a newsagent from Bermondsey aged 35, who had boxed in the 1908 London Olympics, losing in the semi-final to Johnny Douglas, who went on to captain England at cricket.

W. W. Allen, lightweight, a 21-year-old electrician from Kennington.

Alfred Spenceley, a 21-year-old student from Deptford.

It must have been quite an adventure in those times for one so young.

The British team won four of their five fights in Madison Square Garden and the following day the *New York Times* wrote:

> The star of the lot was Ralph Erskine, the 17 year old boy who fights in the 125 pound class. He fought Alfred Roffe, the Canadian champion, and simply toyed with his opponent all through the three rounds. He had all the actions of an experienced performer and the speed of a Jem Driscoll*. He easily outpointed Roffe.

A famous featherweight champion from Cardiff, known as 'Peerless Jem', who fought his way from poverty to the British Championship before dying of consumption in 1925 at the age of 44

The *New York World* wrote that Ralph was 'the best two-handed fighter England had sent across since Charlie Mitchell.' *(A heavyweight prize fighter from Birmingham who had toured the USA in 1889)*

The boxing team returned on the subsequently ill-fated *Lusitania* with Ralph's victory being regarded by many as marking him as the unofficial World Amateur Featherweight Champion, arguably Scotland's first world boxing champion.

In 1913, Ralph enrolled as a medical student at Glasgow University. Dan McKetrick, a leading international boxing promoter, who had organised the American trip, travelled specially to Glasgow to offer Ralph £16,000 *(over 100 times as much in today's values)* to agree to take part in three professional championship fights in America. He knew almost all the boxers of the time, and believed that no man in the world at any weight to which Ralph might grow could beat him. Giving commendable priority to his education, Ralph declined the offer.

The offer was still on the table when the Great War broke out in August 1914. At a special meeting of Clydesdale Harriers, James Erskine as Club Secretary proposed that club operations should be suspended *sine die*. Surplus club funds were subsequently distributed among various war charities.

4

TOMMY

Thomas followed his father's footsteps to Allan Glen's School in Glasgow, starting in 1902 and winning two bursaries, before going to the University of Glasgow in 1908. He took a great many subjects in his time there, spanning the Arts and Sciences, including Logic and History. He also studied Anatomy and Physiology, before studying Medicine from his fifth year in 1912. He lived at home in Tollcross with his father and brother while he studied. Whilst studying, Thomas was a notable athlete and member of the Clydesdale Harriers, and at one point held the post of secretary. He competed in many local sports meetings and occasionally won prizes. At university he was also a Sergeant in the Officer Training Corps.

Writing to Nancy, by then a 16-year-old student at Aberystwyth University, in April 1914, he gave an insight into his views of Welsh and Scottish girls. Nancy had been ill, and he gave her a long lecture about looking after herself, expressing a view which would get him into trouble today.

> Be moderate in everything and avoid undue excitement. Remember that the Welsh girls are of a different

race to us Scots – they are of a more highly strung temperament – and you must guard against their want of balance disturbing your own equilibrium.

After a long discourse on the value of walking as exercise, Tommy continued:

I didn't intend writing so much on this subject, but I hope you will attribute my wordiness to an anxiety on behalf of my wee sister, who we all hope to see growing into a healthy woman. The other type are unfortunately so plentiful – especially among women who have been students – the healthy well-made girls at Queen Margaret's College here are few and far between – the girls seem to lose all self-respect for their physical selves during their student days and then when they graduate after 3 or 4 years they have gained a degree but have often lost much of the freshness of youth and have taxed their bodies to such an extent that they never really regain perfect health

Tommy continues with some family news – Granddaddy had had flu, Ralph had been to Liverpool (by boat!) to see a friend.

I have not been away from home at all this holiday, but have been working a bit each day, usually walking about ten miles in the country in the afternoon. I am feeling fit and well. I was beaten in my Championship fight three weeks ago. It was a close run thing but my opponent, who was an old army boxer, got the decision on points. You will be pleased to know that cousin George Barrie has won the Middleweight Championship of Scotland – the final was last night. It is rather remarkable that

Grandma should have two Scotland champions among her grandsons. I suppose Ralph would have told you about having had the drum of his ear burst. I am glad to say that it has quite healed up now and his hearing is in no way interfered with.

When war broke out, Tommy immediately enlisted in the 4th Battalion Argyll and Sutherland Highlanders. After a period of training in Sunderland, he was commissioned as an officer and attached to the 1st Battalion Gordon Highlanders. A week before Christmas 1914 he joined the regiment in Belgium. After the German advance had been halted at the Battle of the Marne, both sides had dug in to form the Western Front, running from the Channel to the Swiss border. The British Expeditionary Force was responsible for the Belgian sector, including the strategically important Ypres salient. When Tommy joined his battalion, they were holding a position to the east of Kemmel, just south of Ypres. To their north, a Bavarian unit of the German Army was defending a piece of high ground near the village of Wijtschate, known as Hill 80.

Early in 1915, Tommy wrote a long letter to Ralph.

> 1st Gordons, British Expeditionary Force, Belgium.
> Wednesday
>
> Dear Ralph,
>
> At last I have started to write you. Of course I have presumed all along that you were getting my letters to Daddy sent on to you so I felt that to be almost as good as my writing direct to you. You see I seldom feel in a mood to settle down to much writing and sometimes have found it difficult to get even Daddy's letter dispatched. When we are in the trenches we are too

wet and uncomfortable to write, and my time in billets is pretty well occupied. The first two days are spent in getting the mud off ourselves, our clothes and the men's, and the second two in parades, bomb-throwing class (which I take) hurdle making, trench digging and revetting *(constructing a revetment – facing with a layer of stone or concrete or other supporting material so as to retain)* etc.

My company left the fire trenches last night, after two days and nights without a casualty (except for one man who was shot in the hand while going down from the trench to see the doctor at the dressing station having been suffering from dysentery and rheumatics in the trenches). He went down the road where the sniper killed one of my men the other night. We found a road back through the fields last night, and got back to billets without any casualty, which was fairly 'up' the snipers. Yesterday too, we disposed of three German snipers. The one shot first fell over the trench parapet. Another man was seen going to bandage him, and he was promptly potted by one of our crack shots. We had snow and frost in the trenches on Monday, and the weather, though severe, was preferable to the usual rain, into which however, the snow soon turned. On the whole the last 48 hours were the quietest and most uneventful I have yet had in the firing line. There is a marking time at present along our line, as the weather of the last month has made an advance by either side inadvisable. The news from Brigade Headquarters this morning is quite good. The Russians are still doing well and the slight retreat of the French is quite satisfactorily explained by the great floods in the river where they yielded. It is expected that (probably at an early date, and before we get our new armies into the field) the Germans will make another great effort to break through. I only wish they would try it where we are, and we would knock a few of them on top of the line of dead Frenchmen lying out in front of our trench. The Germans in front of our line seem to be strongly ensconced on the ridge of a hill. If we have to take the offensive it will be a stiff job, as we will be fighting uphill. Nevertheless I often, when I look out through the peephole, have a strong desire to be leading my men in a bayonet charge against the position.

At present my company is in a farm 1 ½ miles from the firing line but situated so low as to be pretty secure from German artillery. Besides this is a raw misty day, and unsuited to aeroplane observation of fire. Nevertheless our 18 pounders behind the farm are battering away this afternoon. On Monday night I saw shellfire by night for the first time. For about 15 minutes there was a terrific artillery duel on our left. The shells were bursting in mid-air, each burst being accompanied by a flash of lightning. It was very picturesque, but I'm glad it wasn't to the right, as I had a working party digging a new trench out in the open while the affair was in progress.

I had several of your letters from Daddy and was pleased to get all your news. You were anxious at not receiving word from him. I was very disappointed at not hearing from or receiving a parcel of things I asked for. He has been very busy apparently in his new role as 'wire rope expert' and hence his delay in writing. I expect to find a parcel waiting for me at billets tomorrow night. Re gumboots, if I want them I can indent for them and get them from Headquarters. But they aren't much good as preventives of cold feet in the trenches. We cannot move about at all, and I think numbed feet are inevitable. The officers have tried everything – gumboots, specially made top boots etc and the problem remains unsolved. Boots and puttees, with two pairs of socks on, seem to be as good as anything, so I am sticking to them. Besides, the men have to stick it in those. My feet are practically alright now, and I am feeling 'in the pink', though covered with mud and unshaven.

Dunwiddie, who came to our Company after Gordon was wounded, was a colonel sergeant in Edinburgh OTC *(Officers Training Corps)* and was at Ilkley. He is a nice fellow. I knew his brother better – he was at Glasgow Varsity. Dunwiddie was very weak with diarrhoea after leaving the trenches last night, but is better today. Five new officers have joined us so we aren't so bad. One is a giant – 6 ft 6 and about 16 stone weight – Captain Gordon. I don't envy him in a small dugout.

You asked for particulars of poor Jamie Mylles's death. Well, there is nothing beyond what I said in my letter to Daddy. He was shot by a sniper the first afternoon he was in the trenches – about 3 in the afternoon. The Germans there were only 100 yards away and Jamie must have exposed himself, possibly unknowingly. He was shot through the middle of the brow, and lingered for about 20 minutes only, unconscious. I was only 10 yards away, but couldn't shift from my part of the trench. You can imagine what a shock I got when word came along that he had been shot. I felt sick for an hour or two after. I've got hardened now, however, to such occurrences, although I never wish to be able to regard such a business as this as anything but hellish. Jamie was buried at night, along with one or two other

Gordons, in the little village churchyard at Kemmel. What a shock to his parents, and to Charlie, who has come through so much without a scratch. Jamie had just said to me the previous night that he had a presentiment on the night before that he was going to see Charlie soon. Superstitious or religious people would have interpreted this by saying that Charlie was soon to follow him but Charlie is, as far as I know, still alive and well and I hope he will remain so. (*Lt James Robertson Jack Mylles of the 3rd Battalion Highland Light Infantry was killed on 30 December 1914 aged 21. Charles Mylles, presumably his brother, survived the war.*)

Perhaps as I write this you are on your way to Egypt. It would be fine for getting your men fit again. It's no good bringing anything but trained and fit men out here – they simply go sick immediately. If you go to Egypt, you might see cousin Jack Erskine there.

I'm glad you enjoyed the dance and that the girls were nice. How glorious it will be to get back to sanity again some day – away from the roar of guns and the whish of the beastly snipers – back to bonnie Scotland, home, nice girls, dances and the pleasures of life then made infinitely more sweet. There's much work to be done yet but I feel confident of going through it all right. I don't want to die – I have convinced myself here that life is well worth living – but if I do fall I shall do so in the knowledge that our cause is that of humanity – of right against might.

Have you got into the machine gun section? I hope so. The work offers many opportunities for gaining distinction, but of course is often very dangerous, as the enemy try to shell the gun immediately it is located. Turnbull, one of our lieutenants, got his DSO for saving his machine gun, when wounded, under heavy fire.

I got a letter from Peggy, and one from Jeannie Barrie this week. I also got one from Vera Davies, together with ½lb of chocolate which was very nice and welcome. She is sticking it at Anatomy in this weather. I also got a letter from Madge McDougall, who said she had seen you, and thought you were very like me in looks and in manners. I also had one from Gladys Hillard, a nice little girl I knew at Plymouth – daughter of a naval officer. So that wasn't a bad budget, was it? I haven't had word from you recently, however, so do please write as often as you can. Short and frequent letters will be very welcome – they help to counterbalance the effect of the trenches.

As to 'Hints from the Front', the main things out here are 'a good constitution' and 'good feet' – also of course 'good shooting ability and common sense'. These qualities will make a good soldier – a knowledge of 'book work' is not necessary.

I am glad you had a nice time at home at Christmas. How I should have liked to be there with you all. However, let's hope we shall all be together again next Christmas – with the terror of militarism banished – at least for a long time – from Europe, and good old Scotland still uninvaded.

Yes, one does generally have the feeling out here that he is going to be one of the fortunate. At least I have had it, and the queer thing is that this feeling of confidence increases instead of diminishing when one sees one's friends go. I had a very narrow escape indeed when Gordon was wounded in the farm kitchen, but somehow I was very little perturbed by the event.

I was sorry to hear from Daddy of the death of H.C.D. Ranken RAMC *(Royal Army Medical Corps)*. He was a fine chap and did his recruit drills in the OTC with me – and Teddy Maitland. The old original Company of OTC are doing splendidly indeed.

Daddy's letter came to me in the trenches yesterday – 20 pages, along with four of your letters – I was delighted to get them, and read them with the shells buzzing overhead.

Madge McDougall in her letter says she had a visit from three Canadian kilties, one an Andrew Martin, who was at school with you and knew you well, and who has been in Canada for a year or two. Do you remember him?

Thursday 8.30 am
Another day here and then back to billets and soap and water. The weather today is even worse than usual – dull and wet, so I don't think the Artillery will trouble us much today. We'll leave after dark for billets, which are at a village four miles off.

I enclose the letter from Vera, which you can destroy when you have read it. Please initial my letter and send it on to Daddy to be forwarded to Nancy.

Friday 10.30 am
I have just had a fine breakfast, including porridge. Found parcels waiting for me in billets from Meg Hateley, Jeanie Barrie and Daddy. Cakes, fruit etc. It is a beautiful day – frosty and bright and I am as fit as a fiddle. Am looking forward to a very happy four days till Monday night. Will get anything sent from home thanks. There isn't much you can get out here.

I got a letter from Nancy last night. Have you heard from Lennie recently? Give me all the news.

In haste for post,

Your very loving brother,
Tommy.

The first official record of Tommy's exploits appears in the battalion diary for 4 February 1915.

In trenches near Vierstraat.
A good deal of shelling. Sky full of aeroplanes.

2nd Lieut Erskine (4th A and S Highlanders – attached) saw with his glasses some Germans baling water out of their trenches.

This was communicated to the artillery by telephone with the result that, after the usual ranging shots, a Lyddite Shell, followed in rapid succession by 3 others, was dropped in the middle of them. This incident proves the advantage to be gained by placing the officers in the front trenches in direct touch with the artillery.

For the next two months we are fortunate to have some extensive diary entries recording Tommy's activities and feelings.

On 8 February 1915 he was in billets in a village called La Clytte and having a reasonably relaxed time.

10.30 pm
Our second day in billets has been a very pleasant one. The weather was fine. In the morning our company bathed across the way and in the afternoon I took the bomb class. McCallum is to go down to St Omer on Sat for a fortnight's training in machine gun. He and I have just been to dinner with Major Baird, the Commanding Officer, tonight. Among other good things we had

partridge. The C.O. is a fine man – an ideal leader. His whole care is the welfare of his Battalion – and of course its fighting efficiency. He is a man to inspire confidence in his subordinates. He always speaks what he thinks – whether to subordinates or superiors – he doesn't knuckle down to anyone – even to the General. I believe he gave our Divisional General a terrible telling off after the glorious but expensive charge of the 14th. General Haldane made all sorts of promises re the Gordons, but the Major told him that nothing would bring back his brave men who had been lost. He was left in command of a Brigade in the firing line at Ypres and did brilliant work, being mentioned in dispatches often, and getting his DSO. I would go anywhere at his bidding.

This afternoon we played 'C' Company for the third time, as they weren't satisfied with two defeats. We beat them this time by 4-1. I played inside right for 'A' Company.

I took the 7.15 parade this morning, so Dunwiddie will take it tomorrow. As I am tired now, however, I'm off to bed.

Two days later Tommy performed in a concert held in the barn.

10.30 pm
Just a brief note before bed. I had rather a busy day today. I was along at Cherpenburg all forenoon with a party cutting brushwood and in the afternoon used the material for making fascines *(bundles of rods or pipes bound together for strengthening the sides of ditches or trenches)* for the trenches.

We had another successful concert in our company barn. McCallum, who dined with us, Morrison, Dunwiddie and myself each contributed to the programme. I gave a short parody composed by me today to the air of 'The Wearing o' the Green'. It was very well received.

Cunningham, who has just come in from Headquarters, tells me I am to attend a Court of Enquiry tomorrow at 9 am at Brigade Headquarters. Most of the day will be spent by the company in getting ready to move off for the trenches at 6.15 pm (the hour is getting later each time in billets, as we don't leave La Clytte till dusk, so that it will be dark when we get near the firing line).

I'm going off to bed now, leaving Dunwiddie to make up some arrears in his correspondence.

Tommy's next entry illustrated the ruthlessness of the military discipline of the time.

Wednesday 4 pm
The Court of Enquiry occupied the forenoon. The other members of the board were a Captain and a lieutenant of the Royal Scots. The subject was a Gordon who came out with the last draft. He was shot in the foot while cleaning his rifle in his billet barn. You see the rifles always have 5 rounds in the magazine. We found his wound was 'self-inflicted due to carelessness' so he will get a Court Martial. He'll probably get off lightly as there is no suggestion of 'intention' in his case. Four men who went asleep on sentry duty last time we were in the trenches were very fortunate to get off with 4 years penal each – I thought they might be shot. I'm

glad they weren't however, and hope their case will be a warning to the men who have come out recently. This is a dry day and promises fairly well for our spell in the trenches. We go to No 1 reserve Farm for 48 hours – the 'Gordon' farm – and then to the 2nd firing line.

No word from Daddy for some time – I wonder why. Had a letter from Minnie today.

Tommy had a couple of quiet days before going back into the trenches.

Thursday 8 pm
We've had a very quiet and peaceful day.

Friday 6 pm
Another quiet day, nothing untoward having happened. We are waiting for rations to arrive, and after they are distributed we go off to the firing line, where we remain till Sunday night. We are almost glad to be going into the trenches as we have spent the last two days in this farm kitchen which is quite dark owing to the barricaded windows and very draughty due to the cracks in the doors.

His return to the trenches brought a little action.

Sunday 11 am
Yesterday was such a miserable day that I couldn't be bothered doing anything but lie low in the dry part of my dugout. This was the place I took such pains to make comfortable and since I was last here it was half burned down owing to the carelessness of a Suffolk officer or

his servant. It has been patched up but is not nearly as weather-proof as it was. After raining most of the day yesterday it cleared up in the evening. About 10 o'clock, after issue of rations, I got my men on to work, some at parapet improvement, others to pump the water out of the trenches. The pump was going well and (when it isn't clogged up) is very useful.

Captain Marshall, who is in the trenches in front with D Company, sent for me several times during the night to fire off some bombs (rifle grenades) in the direction of German working parties audible in front, and also at the sniper who lies not very far in front of our left machine gun. At 2 o'clock I wakened my platoon sergeant, who then came on duty and I slept a bit before stand to at 5.30 (although I was called over by Marshall at 4 30). The sniping was very heavy last night, but luckily we had no casualties. Several bullets however whizzed within inches of my head. At the moment it is raining heavily and looks like doing so all day. There is one blessing – the artillery will be quiet.

After this spell in the firing line, Tommy's unit returned to billets, where an artillery duel took place.

Monday 3 pm
There was some excitement last night after all before the battalion got back to billets.

Between four and five there was a very severe artillery battle, all the batteries on both sides banging away. The shells from those on the right were whizzing over our heads in quick succession but bursting a bit behind our trenches although a Jack Johnson* burst just in front of our trench and one just behind. When we got back to billets we heard that the 28th Division (consisting of British regiments who came from India – including the 1st A and S Highlanders) had been broken through but had taken the trenches again by a counter attack. The heavy artillery fire was due to the fact that our guns were supporting our attack. The scene of the battle is about ½ mile to our left.

Just after dark a message came through the phone that I was to get back at once to headquarters to take over some grenades and bombs (the Adjutant was afraid to truck them in case they explode). I just got home with the first company and was back in billets by 9.15. My company didn't arrive till about 11 pm. It turned out that as they were coming down the road from the firing line a heavy fire was opened up by the Germans and they had to squat down in the ditch by the roadside until things quietened a bit. The bullets were whacking and rebounding on the road beside them bespattering them with mud, but by a miracle no one was hit and the whole battalion got back to billets without a single casualty in the 4 days – a record.

It was 12.30 before we got to bed and we didn't breakfast till 10 this morning. This, being the first in billets, is an easy day.

A 'Johnson' was the nickname given to German 12lb shells which were black. The name – which today would not be politically correct – derived from the famous World Heavyweight Boxing Champion Jack Johnson, who was the first African American to hold the title.

From the morning's news we learn that the Russians have had to retreat before the supreme effort of the Germans but a strategic reason is given for this retreat which seems quite satisfactory. If the Germans are checked this time it will have a great effect on the Eastern situation. The Russians have been doing splendidly. The Germans are being dumped on every hand. The state of affairs in Germany is very satisfactory from our point of view.

On returning to the trenches, Tommy complained about the previous occupants.

Sat 9 am
Owing to a rearrangement of trenches, our battalion went into the firing line a day early. Since our company had been last in the fire trenches, we had been out of them only 3 days, and as Wed night was very wet and miserable, we were relieved on Thursday night by C Company and came to this 2nd reserve farm. We go back to La Clytte tonight and don't go back to trenches till next Wed.

Our luck hasn't been so good this time. We had two killed and three wounded. We caught a party of 6 Germans about 30 yards in front of our trench in the dark. They were either out to cut our barbed wire or to throw grenades into our trenches. If the latter was their intention we were lucky to have caught them in time. We gave them a few rounds rapid and killed two of them. The others got away but some are probably wounded.

From last night we take over another length of trench on our right. It holds 150 men, so that means another company in the firing line. I don't know whether this entails longer stretches for us in the trenches at a time. Unfortunately the Honourable Artillery Company (HAC) has occupied the new trench for some time and they have apparently made no attempt to drain or improve it. That means that we have all the donkey work to start again to make it habitable. These damned fools have been wasting thousands of rounds of ammunition replying aimlessly to the German snipers. They have had regular battles (with only themselves firing) every night keeping those on their right and left (us) from resting, with the result that if they are attacked some night we may mistake the noise for one of their regular fusillades. It's a case of 'crying wolf' again. Their officers must be a useless lot, and the men very nervy.

Tommy's complaints are backed up by the Regimental Diary for 19 February 1915, which recorded:

Cold, some rain. In the evening the battalion handed over part of the line of trenches it was holding to the 2nd Royal Scots, taking over in its place a trench known as K2 from the Honourable Artillery Company. This proved to be a very bad bargain as the trench taken over was found to be in a most deplorable condition. Such work as had been done on it appears to have been largely devoted to the provision of shelters, making the place resemble an Indian bazaar. These shelters were so placed as to reduce the fighting value of the parapet to an almost negligible quantity.

At the weekend Tommy had some time off and used it for an expedition in which he came across a funeral service.

Wed 11 am

Have made no entry in diary since Saturday. I have either been too busy working or too busy resting. On Sunday afternoon Dunwiddie and I left here at 2 pm to walk to Ypres, about 5 miles away. We got to Dickebusch – a distance of 3 miles – and found the 1st Argyll and Sutherland and 1st Camerons there. Preparations were being made for the burial of two officers – Lieut Stirling of A and S Highlanders, and Lieut Dunsmure of Camerons, who had been killed the previous afternoon. The men were turned out with reversed arms, the officers of each regiment, from COs down, were present and the scene was very impressive. I heard that Captain Chrystal, my old captain in the 4th at Sunderland was with the 1st, but his company happened to be up in the Reserve Firing Line. I was keen to see him so I left D to have tea in Dickebusch and I made my way along hedges towards the firing line. I found Chrystal and his subaltern Lieut Steele living in the cellar of a ruined Belgian mansion house. The company were in dugouts in the grounds of the house. What a beautiful residence it must have been before the war – painted white with fine pillars and architecture. Chrystal was delighted to see me and I to see him. Not only so, but I saw quite a number of my old Sunderland platoon who have come out with drafts. My old platoon sergeant Charlie Harkness I found among Chrystal's lot, still as cheery as ever.

A week ago when we were in billets the 9th Brigade passed through La Clytte on its way to strengthen the

27th Div where they had been broken through. I stood at the door of our billet and watched them pass. I saw Laird, of the 1st Royal Scots Fusiliers (I knew he was there) but further down the column of the same regiment who should I meet but wee Mayberry, also of the OTC whom I saw last at Gilmorehill. Further back in the column came V.B.Hill, the varsity and international hockey player. He had been wounded and had come out again with a draft of Northumberland Fusiliers.

I was delighted to see Charlie Mylle's name in Kitchener's dispatch list. Of course I looked for it with confidence that it would be there. They couldn't avoid giving him it, for he's come through the thick and thin. If higher distinctions weren't so hard to get in this war he would have got a DSO. Several officers of this battalion were mentioned, including Bartholomew, captain of the Edinburgh Univ Hares and Hounds, who was first man for Scotland in the race at Ilkley in 1913. B has been home on sick leave and is back again, but looking none too well. Very few of the officers who came through the early dark days of the war are still the same physically as they were before. Most of them have had their nerves more or less shattered.

Now the weather deteriorated as Tommy's unit had a brief respite before returning to the firing line.

3 pm
After several beautiful days the rain is simply pouring down. Luckily our company goes into 1st reserve farm for two nights, but the company in the firing line will have a rotten time. It may clear up before we go to the trenches.

There has been very heavy firing all day up in the Ypres direction, the big guns have been booming incessantly. We had rather a bad time in the trenches last time – 3 men killed, 7 men and 1 officer wounded.

Wed 24 Feb 11 pm
We arrived at reserve farm about nine covered in snow, there having been a blinding snowstorm since we left billets. Under the new arrangement of reserve trenches one platoon and one officer have to stay at a farm further along the road, so Dunwiddie and no 4 platoon were detailed. Cunningham and I had just got some food when word came that 1 officer and 38 men were required to go and relieve the Suffolks in trench L6, the platoon of C company which should have relieved them having lost their way, or at least not having arrived. I had to harness myself at once and scoot. We got to the firing line in record time but met the Suffolks, having been relieved, coming away. We doubled back as quick as we could to the farm here. It was no thanks to C Company that we didn't have any casualties as the German brutes were sniping heavily and the bullets whizzed by our heads as we came across the fields.

Tommy was then sick for a few days but not before he had demonstrated remarkable marksmanship.

Friday 5 March
It is more than a week since my last entry in the diary. The Battalion went into the trenches last night, but I am missing this tour. I went to bed on Wed night with some temperature (the doctor didn't say how much) as the result of a cold contracted in my last dugout where

my bed consisted of an old spring mattress placed on an old wooden door which in turn was floating in water. It was bloody. I knew I was contracting something but the trench pump wouldn't work and the water had to stay. Our company had only one casualty last time, and that was sustained at the last moment, a man was killed after being relieved – when he had got 20 yards behind the trench. We had some narrow escapes with shrapnel. The Germans aimed 15 shells in succession on my little part of trench. They all 'just missed' however, although two burst right on top of my dugout and made me 'hug the leeward'. I think I mentioned before that the General promised to give our C.O. a telescopic rifle to be tried by me on the group of Germans I had seen so often but who were too far away to be vulnerable to ordinary rifle fire. Well that rifle is now in my possession. I had a great afternoon in the trenches with it last week. I killed at least one German (shot him through the head at 900 yards with strong wind blowing), possibly two, and may have wounded others. I just missed getting an officer. It was great to see them looking about wondering where the shots were coming from. They have a telescopic rifle to every 8 men you know. Hence the accuracy of their sniping.

The Suffolks are now in the village, having been relieved by us last night. One of the officers has been in bed all day next door, so this house is a hospital pro-tem. A young officer aged 19 who always billeted in this house was killed, it seems, on Monday. I see Mayberry the OTC man in the Royal Scottish Fusiliers, who passed through the village 3 weeks ago, is home wounded already. He was a great pal of Gordon at the Varsity.

This is the first time I've missed the trenches since I came out, but it was better to miss them once now than to have to go properly sick later on. I intend getting out tomorrow and hope to be as fit as ever by our next turn. Besides it's rather nice to have a rest and a day or two in bed after three months continuous duty. I am Transport Officer in the village till the battalion returns, having to visit the transport lines once a day to see that the stables etc are clean and ok. Not a hard job, eh? If I feel strong tomorrow I may ride as far as Ypres on Sunday.

Reinforcements arrived in the shape of a detachment of Territorial troops.

Sat 6 pm
Have been up since midday. Got Mackay to spring-clean my little attic and it was badly needed too. Have been writing letters all afternoon. The RQMs *(Regimental Quarter Masters)* told me that the British had 3 killed the first day in the trenches yesterday and 2 were in A Company. These snipers do kill or miss. I hope the other 3 days won't be so bad. This has been another wet day and I was glad I wasn't in the trenches.

The 4th Gordons (Territorials) have arrived now and are being broken into the trenches by going one company at a time with our other battalions. I was over some days ago on three occasions giving them lessons on grenade and bomb throwing and they were very much impressed and interested. They are a fine lot of men, but their officers of course are only typical Territorial Officers and their discipline is not too good. However 'the proof's in the preeing'. *('to pree – old Scottish slang; to try by tasting)*

Back in the firing line, Tommy endured a pretty uncomfortable couple of days.

> Tuesday 2 pm
>
> Here we are again! I'm miles behind with my diary, but must just make the best of it. We are due to go back to billets tonight, but there is a rumour of us having to remain on duty longer and in that case my company would be relieved by another company of our regiment instead of by the Suffolks and we would just go back again to support farm. I hope not however. I've had a pretty strenuous time this time, having done actually three days in the trenches. Our first two days we were in reserve, but the C.O. sent me up to occupy, with two other men, a new trench which had been dug by sappers in the dark, but which had never been occupied by day, and the nature of the 'position' value of which was unknown. I had been up at the firing line from 12 till 2 with a working party. Having dossed on the straw in the farm kitchen for 2 hours, I was up again at 4 am and had to trek a way up to get into the new trench before daylight. I found it narrow and, having found the only comfortably dry part of it, I, Mackay and McKnight sat on our packs, just under cover all day. My shoulders were hard up against the sides, making it difficult to turn round, so I couldn't be bothered preparing any food. We had one meal – about midday – cold bully beef, bread and an apple (which I shared with the men). At dusk about 6.30 we trekked back to the farm.

But his route to the trenches had not been without incident.

> Re the first journey to the trenches that night – several sappers in the charge of a corporal were to take us to a

new trench to dig. I had 25 of my own men with me. The sapper corporal and I went in front, he guiding. After much trouble finding gaps in barbed wire and having been on the way for about an hour the sapper corporal confessed to me that he'd lost his way. Not knowing the lie of that bit myself there was nothing for it but to take my men back and report the affairs to our C.O. I didn't blame the corporal much, as it turned out he'd only been in the trench once and in that case shouldn't have been sent to guide us at all. It was very dark and only one well acquainted with a path can follow it these dark moonless nights. But I was annoyed next day to hear from the C.O. that the corporal sapper had said the Gordons officer had taken the party back because there was too much sniping. I saw a sapper officer over at our headquarters farm next night, Major Baird having sent for me, and I cleared the matter up. The corporal will be reduced to the ranks, and is lucky at that, as I might have charged him with cowardice. There was some considerable sniping, undoubtedly, and we were more likely to be hit because of the slowness of our progress. Indeed I have no doubt that the corporal's tardy advance was due as much to funk as to ignorance of the way. Several times I had to make the whole line lie flat and the corporal was always first down. One time two bullets in succession struck a post beside us, and the corporal disappeared with a splash into a ditch full of water. I make great allowance for these sappers, they are only territorials and their officers are just engineers – not soldiers – some aren't even the former. The discipline etc is non-existent but they do some fairly useful work up round the trenches and in the billet villages. The joke of the matter was that next day in daylight I saw that the place where we had turned the previous night was only about 300 yards from the trench we had been making for. Had I known where the trench lay I could have taken the party up myself in 20 minutes by a direct route.

Tommy's next entry described in more detail the difficulties of a night advance.

I led our company up from the farm to the trenches on Sunday night. Our route varies according to the section of the trench we are going to. We go cross-country all the way, and the chief difficulty lies in leading through the gaps in the barbed wire entanglements which stretch across the fields behind the firing line and also over the narrow bridges across the narrow canals which abound here. The fields are covered with 'Krump' and 'Johnson' holes, mostly full of water. The leader simply gropes his way forward, feeling for holes etc with a stick. The company stretches out in a long single file behind. The German flares come right over behind the firing line, often lying at our feet and showing up the whole company. When that occurs we all stand motionless until the light dies away. Sometimes if we are spotted we squat down till the volley of bullets ceases – they often whack into the ground beside us. The continual flaring is really a hindrance to progress on a dark night – after the brightness dies away one's dazzled eyes can see nothing but blackness in front. Well on Sunday night I undertook for the captain to lead the company straight as a die from the farm to the K trenches here. I took a new road which I had previously noted – almost dead straight across the country, and led them right up to the very trench. The path all the way was bone dry and we walked straight through the wire gaps and across the bridges without difficulty. It was rather a successful piece of night trekking. Of course there is always the odd man behind who doesn't follow the leader exactly and goes over the knees in a hole. The new moon was due last night, so next time we come back we'll just have a nice light.

So much for that. I forgot to mention rather an exciting time we had late on Sunday afternoon before we left the Reserve Farm. Suddenly, about 4.30 pm, just as we (the officers) were at tea in the kitchen there was a sound as of a storm rising – a whizzing as of a sudden wind. In a moment the shells were bursting all round the farm house. In another our artillery was answering back, and there ensued a terrific artillery duel. Our company was immediately ordered out of the barns into the dug-outs. There was rapid fire heard up from the trenches, and we thought the Germans must be delivering an attack. We were ordered to hold ourselves ready to go at dusk if the bombardment continued, and take our places in the 2nd line of trenches. A most terrific cannonade was kept up for an hour and a quarter, and by some miracle we didn't have a casualty although the slates were being brought down from the roofs of the buildings and barns beside us, and the shells were bursting everywhere. All our guns behind were going full pelt and ultimately, having established a superiority of fire of at least 3 to 1, they silenced the German guns altogether and we went back to finish our tea. It turned out next morning that the Germans had taken some of our trenches at St Eloi (2 miles away). Their game had been to keep us on the hop and prevent us sending support along to there. We retook all the trenches (except two small pieces) next night. There had been no infantry attack on our trenches.

The battalion diary recorded:

Fine day with mist. About 5.15 pm a heavy bombardment by Germans commenced (attack on St Eloi), which lasted about 1½ hours. At 7 pm orders received to cancel move ordered the previous day. At 8 pm orders received to carry on with the new move and finally at 9 pm fresh orders were received cancelling the move. Inter-company reliefs consequently took place and were not complete until 2.45 am. Quiet night, 3 men wounded.

Then a daring night raid.

I had rather a tricky job on hand last night. I, with two men in my platoon (time-serving men who have been out since the beginning) crawled out over a hundred yards in front of our barbed wire. We lay flat and I sent 5 rifle grenades into the German trenches. Each time I fired I drew the rifle fire and flares of the German trenches. Several flares landed just beside us and showed us up very plainly to our own people behind. But of course they knew where to look for us. When the flares were up we lay flat as if dead, and the Germans didn't spot us, being unable to distinguish us from the dead men around us. (We found a dead German lying beside us.) We watched the flash of the rifle of a sniper about 150 yards in front of us and I put the grenades in his direction. I hope I got someone in the trench. I think I did, as they all went off well and just where I aimed them. We lay out for an hour and a half watching and listening for a German patrol – but no advance parties came forward. In going back we landed at a trench 100 yards along the line from our own (it's so easy to lose one's direction when crawling). Luckily we had warned the other trenches that we were out or we might have been shot for Germans.

Then the battalion suffered some dreadful casualties.

Wed 8 pm

We had as a battalion to do an extra day on duty on account of the thinning of the line by the recent fighting at St Eloi, where it seems we had some 1000 casualties in taking some 3000 yards of ground. Our company therefore, when relieved last night from the trenches, came into Support Farm instead of going back to La Clytte. The extra day on duty has proved a disastrous one for us. We've had no casualties here since Gordon was wounded 2 months ago. Today however the Germans shelled us with shrapnel. Very heavily. By some miracle a shell went into the door of one of the barns, killing 5 men and wounding 11 on the spot. We had a terrible time bandaging the wounded. The tragedy occurred about 2 o'clock and the men had to be waiting all afternoon for dusk when they were carried back to the dressing station. The dead men are being buried now out behind the farm. Three of them were in a terrible condition. Their heads had all been blown off leaving the trunks mangled and the flesh and blood splattered against the wall. It was a terrible sight. As usual too, some of the remaining old hands suffered – 2 out of the 5 killed came out with the battalion and had been through thick and thin with it. Another had just returned with the last draft – having been wounded. The terrible feature of this being shelled in buildings is that one doesn't have any chance of retaliating – we don't know which guns behind the hill are having us – we just wait in suspense till it's over and it's a pure lottery whether one escapes or not. We had just been congratulating ourselves on having no casualties in the firing line in our company – and then we had 16 in one fell swoop – and we really ought to have been back at La Clytte today. Such are the fortunes of war. I've had my bellyful of blood today, I can tell you. One couldn't but admire the manner in which the wounded men, some of them very seriously and perhaps fatally hit, lay patiently suffering all afternoon behind the farm waiting for the stretcher bearers.

One of those poor fellows today had been set on fire by the shell, and the ammunition in his pouches was going off in the barn. A pail of water had to be thrown over him to extinguish the flames and his body was all charred when I saw him. Ugh! War is a hellish business. The Sgt Major has just come in to tell me that Bruce, one of the wounded, died before arrival at the dressing station. He suffered terribly all afternoon and was continually asking for water, his throat being apparently parched. I didn't like the look of him – his face had a death-like pallor and I thought he was doomed. Well that's 6 dead so far – not a bad little toll for one shell.

We are waiting for the Suffolks to relieve us and we won't be sorry to get back to billets tonight. I hope we'll manage without further casualties – the snipers are busy at present and many of the bullets are striking the farm or whizzing across the courtyard.

Then back to new trenches.

Friday 5 pm

After only two days in billets we are going up to take over new trenches near St Eloi where the heavy fighting has been going along. I wonder when we'll get a rest. Yet we're not so badly off as some. Today's papers show the Camerons to have lost 14 officers killed and 8 wounded – in that business at Neuve Chapelle. It seems to have been a terrible affair. The Germans would need to have lost treble as many as we have or I can't see that it can have been worth our while to have advanced so little at so great a cost. The 1st A and S H (Argyll and Sutherland Highlanders) must have been in the scrap, as Lieut Steele, who was Chrystal's subaltern when I saw him a month ago, has been killed. A fine young fellow he was, very strong and powerful looking. Chrystal would probably be out of it, as he was transferred to the 2nd A and SHs.

We had a fire in our billets here today, the main barn in which ¾ of our company lodged being burned to the ground. If we come back to La Clytte (which is doubtful) we will need to find a new farm.

Cooking was quite a challenge.

Monday 22 March 2 pm

We came out of trenches last night, and are now in a support farm just behind. The dwelling part of the farm has been wiped out by shell, but the barns have solid brick roofs (supported by iron girders) which seem to have so far remained unpierced. We are quite safe from ordinary shrapnel here, but high explosive shrapnel or Johnson would get us. A couple of the former burst on the front (unoccupied) end of the farm in the forenoon and we were afraid we were in for it again, but in the succeeding rounds they 'switched off' further along the road, thereby indicating that this farm was not their target. I hope they won't find out that we're using this place for support – as we are likely to be occupying this section of the line for some time.

We have no kitchen here at all and we (the officers) are occupying pens in a stable barn, like a lot of cattle. We can't have any coke fires during daylight, as the slightest vestige of smoke escaping outside would be at once spotted by the hawks eyes of the enemy's observers and we would be showered with shells. However, by dint of careful stoking, we managed to boil two canteens of water on a small fire made in a bully beef tin and stoked with thin shavings of wood so as to make no smoke. We had a good breakfast of tea, tinned veal and boiled eggs. We won't get any more food cooked till after dark (about 8 at the earliest).

The new positions had a legacy left by the French.

Well, about our new trenches. They are much nearer the Germans than our last were. Indeed my section, which is the most forward, is only 40 yards from the Germans. Their trench is just on the outside of a small wood and mine less than a stone's throw across. You can guess how careful we had to be. All lookouts by day use periscopes, and the latter mustn't be used for more than a few seconds at a time or it will be spotted and shot at. My periscope was shot twice, each time right through the thin wooden stem. Of course we reach our trench under cover by communication trenches. The French occupied this position for a long time, and seem to have made several unsuccessful attempts at further advance as their dead are scattered all over the place. To my right is a regular row of 25 corpses about 5 yards in front of our trenches. The French evidently tried to advance and had a machine gun turned on them, mowing them down in a line.

After a brief respite, they were back in the trenches again – Tommy discussed the casualties at the Battle of Neuve Chapelle.

Wed

We went back to a support farm on Sunday 4 pm and returned to the firing line last night, so that of the last 10 days we have spent only 2 in billets. There is no prospect of a relief yet – there doesn't seem to be a battalion to take our place here at present. We go back to reserve farm tomorrow night, and after 2 days there we will return again to the firing line unless the battalion is relieved. I hope they'll give us a longer spell in billets when it does come – we're ready for a rest now. This is the longest spell in the trenches the battalion has had since Ypres.

I have here a paper of 22nd inst. giving another list of casualties of Neuve Chapelle. Our 2nd battalion has lost most of its officers including its colonel. Poor Tommy Letters, the cheery clever fellow of Glasgow University, whom Ralph and I often spoke about, is reported 'missing, believed killed'. It's terrible. Captain Halliswell HLI *(Highland Light Infantry)* is wounded. I wonder if Charlie Mylles got through it. It's a piece of pure good fortune that our battalion didn't happen to be in this show. There were 517 casualties among officers alone. The Germans yesterday put a rifle grenade into the trench on our right, killing 1 officer and wounding 6 men

– of the Suffolk Regiment. I hope my grenades have accounted for a good many of the enemy.

Tommy described life in a redoubt.

I am this time in charge of a small party of 215 men in a redoubt which is situated in a small wood about 200 yards behind the firing trench. It forms a sort of support trench. The enemy aren't supposed to know that we are here, so our main object is to retain its secrecy. We lie doggo in dugouts all day and move about by night. It's a long day from dawn at 5 am till dusk about 7.30 but we doss most of the forenoon at least. It's a regular rodent's life this – living in holes by day and showing ourselves only by night. It's rather a good little post this however. The enemy don't shell it and we are protected from rifle fire by a little mound on which the wood stands.

After a long spell of dry weather we have had two wet days. The trench in the wood here is in a terribly muddy state.

McCallum evacuated this dugout last night, and left 'The Isle of Unrest' by Henry Seton Merryman, for me to read. I had breakfast about 8 am – bacon and eggs and have had nothing else but a little chocolate. We cannot relight our coke fires till dusk – lest the smoke be seen by the enemy – and so we won't have tea till after 8.

Although the shells are hustling through the air incessantly, the birds are whistling in the trees above – heedless of everything except the advent of spring. How I envy them.

This last observation – redolent of the poem *In Flanders Fields* – is the final entry of the diary which survives.

A summary of Tommy's observations was published in *The Glasgow Herald* of 2 April 1915 and is in Appendix A.

In May 1915 Tommy's battalion was relocated a few miles to the east of Ypres close to a feature called Hill 60. This was a small artificial hill which had been created in the previous century with spoil from the construction of the local railway line. Although only about 60 feet high, it had considerable strategic value as it commanded views of Ypres and its surroundings. It changed hands several times early in the war before being recaptured by the Germans in April 1915 with the first use of gas in the war.

The battalion diary for May and June 1915 recorded:

> 11 May. Orders received in evening that battalion will move at 2 pm tomorrow to relieve 13th Brigade in front of Hill 60.

> 12 May. Battalion marched off at 1.30 pm and halted in Chateau grounds SSW of Ypres till 7 pm. Relieved South Lancs in trenches encircling Hill 60. *(Hooge Chateau was a local manor house.)*

> 28 May. Occupied new position near Hooge.

> 9 June. Gas training.

Then, more seriously:

> 15 June. Gassed. Equipment effective.

On the following two nights Tommy was in action.

16 June. Many wounded from other units were found in trenches but all were sent back or brought under cover.

Lieut Erskine discovered that trenches 250 yards in front of us were unoccupied. It was decided to occupy them at dusk and this was done without any opposition.

17 June. Trenches were much improved during the night and approaches blocked by Lieuts Erskine and Horsley with bomb throwers. Several gas shells used by enemy.

The following day the battalion was relieved and had some rest time at Brandhoek, just to the west of Ypres. There was even time for a football match, in which they beat Liverpool Scottish 6-2, and a visit to the baths in nearby Poperinge.

Tommy's various activities led to his being mentioned in dispatches and, after a Sunday morning church parade on 11 July, he was presented with the Military Cross, then the second highest military bravery award after the Victoria Cross.

The citation read:

Lieutenant Thomas Barrie Erskine, 4th Battalion, Princess Louise's (Argyll and Sutherland Highlanders), attached 1st Battalion, The Gordon Highlanders. For conspicuous gallantry and ability. Between 12th and 20th May, 1915, he obtained definite information of the enemy's dispositions near 'Hill 60' by personal reconnaissance by day and night, and, after locating the enemy's nearest occupied trench from a distance of 10 to 20 yards, he checked their activities by incessantly bombing their working parties. His work was marked by equal boldness and judgment. He has also shown since conspicuous energy and skill in the construction of defences in Hooge Village.

Just over a week later, on 19 July, Tommy was selected for a permanent commission and promoted to captain. We can only hope he was told of this because on the same evening Tommy took part in what was to be his final action.

The Battalion Diary gives the overall picture.

19/20 July

About 10 pm orders received for Headquarters and two companies to proceed to Ypres ramparts as soon as possible. On arrival a carrying party took bombs to the front trenches at Hooge where they were urgently required. A mine had been exploded by us at 7 pm under a German redoubt under Bull Farm and an attack was delivered by the Middlesex Regiment assisted by our grenadiers, snipers and machine gunners on this front and in the adjacent trenches. This attack was quite successful, the crater of the mine being occupied and about 80 yards of German trenches to the west being captured. The losses among the grenadiers, snipers and machine gunners amounted to killed 9, wounded 34 and included Lt TB Erskine, 4th Argyll and Sutherland Highlanders who was killed: this officer was transferred by gazette a few days later – his loss was mourned deeply by the battalion by all ranks of which he was a favourite. 2/Lt Horsley who was in charge of the snipers was also wounded.

The diary doesn't tell the whole story.

Tommy was the Bombing Officer, which involved lobbing grenades into the deadly enemy machine-gun dug-out posts. *Great War Magazine*, a large circulation weekly publication of the time described the action more fully:

> During a difficult and thrilling charge near the famous Hooge Chateau, a party of bombers led by Lieut T Erskine, came to a dug-out in which some Germans were barricaded and refused to surrender. It was defended by a breastwork against which the bombs could make no impression. Despite a fierce cross-fire, he seized a pickaxe and started to hew a way into the dug-out. While doing this, he was mortally wounded with a shot through the chest. He died of his wounds in a field ambulance the following day.

This act of extraordinary, even insane, bravery is captured in an illustration in the same magazine. Tommy is depicted as wearing a kilt; this was common practice for Scottish regiments, who found them more practical for wading through mud.

Tommy was recommended for a Distinguished Service Order, the commendation reading:

> This officer led the bombers on the left attack on the German trenches at Hooge on 19 July 1915 and was the first man into the enemy's lines; he set a splendid example of courage and coolness to his men and led them with great gallantry until he was wounded.

Despite this commendation being signed by no less than General Allenby, for some reason this award never materialised – a cause of great angst to Granddaddy as we shall see later.

A few days later Granddaddy wrote to Nancy, his grief only too raw.

My darling Nancy,

It is too true! Our dear Tommy is dead. We shall never see him again. Never hear his beloved voice. I am distracted with grief. I cry incessantly within myself – 'My son! My son! Would to God that I had died for thee!' But nothing avails. He is dead, and will not return to us. My son, my brother, my friend! All the world mourns with us; but – there is no return. Oh, Nancy, I have no consolation to offer you except that he loved you dearly and that he has left a memory fragrant of everything brave and good and lovely. If you had only seen him when he was here a month ago! I had no means of communicating with you and time was so short. He was happy and cheerful and looked so big and strong that everybody felt cheered by having seen him. Dr Kerr wrote to me after he went away – 'What a heroic figure is Tom'. All who met him felt the suggestion of solidity and strength – mentally and spiritually as well as bodily – and of potential heroism.

And now, Nancy, it is Ralph, our other hero, and Jack and Jamie and the millions of brave boys who are carrying on Tommy's work, that we must think of, and so perhaps achieve a little forgetfulness of Tommy's loss. I have been so absorbed in my own worries that I have neglected to reply to Minnie's letters to me. Tell her I am sorry.

I was in London up till a week ago, calling at the War Office to rectify their mistakes in connection with my application for a commission. I am at last being appointed to a Lieutenancy in the 7th Gordons and expect to leave for Semi Camp near Perth in a day or two. I was very happy about it; but now – it is different. I have not heard any particulars of Jamie's appointment, nor any recent news of Jack. I hope both are well and that Uncle John and Aunt Maggie and Minnie and Mabel (and Wharfi) are all in good health. They will be sad enough and anxious enough too; but I hope they will never suffer as we are doing. Give them all my love.

I would like to see you before I go to Perth; but that may be impossible. If you are coming to Glasgow on your way to Auchterarder (if you are going this week) you might wire me. Uncle Tom Coupar has invited me to go to Girvan (South Ayrshire) for a couple of days but I'm afraid I cannot go, although I am very much in need of a change. Betty and I may sail to Lamlash (Isle of Arran) tomorrow instead. Uncle Tom Barrie's family is there.

Write to me soon, dear.
Your loving
Daddy

(Betty was a companion who made intermittent appearances in Granddaddy's life. Her name was Betty Chalmers and she worked as a purser on a Canadian shipping line, so her appearances in Glasgow were sporadic. She was described as 'a rather intense, unprepossessing bespectacled lady'.)

Writing from France, Ralph was equally upset and concerned for his younger sister.

My wee sister Nancy,

This is a great grief that has fallen us. Our Tommy is dead. Our brother, so good and noble. I can weep no more and now the light has gone out of my life. But we mustn't allow ourselves to be despondent, we must fight the fight to the end. My great fear is that the grief will be too much for Daddy. You must see him as often as you can to comfort him. Who has a better right? If you are at Auchterarder he should be fairly close at Scone. You and I must try to fill the gap.

And I, now, shall be very careful for his dear sake and yours. We must try to forget because no good can come of brooding. And when you do think of it remember that our Tommy died like a hero. If I could only have died for him. He was so much better than I. But these things are in the lap of the Gods.

The work with the regiment should help Daddy to forget, but he must never come out here. It would never do. Now Nancy dear write often so that we can be as near to each other as possible.

Your loving brother,

Ralph

Other letters of condolence poured in.

Mary Lee, Nancy's future sister-in-law, writing from Wilmslow in Cheshire:

Nancy Dear,

Words absolutely fail me to try and express how very, very deeply I feel for you in this overwhelming sorrow.

Little did I think (when we parted only a few hours ago) that mother would have such sad news for me on my return. It is just too terrible and I feel for you more than I can say.

To think after your brother's wonderful bravery, he should not live to receive the MC.

Although it is all so sad dear, how proud you must feel that you have had such a brave and true brother. His name will go down in the list of England's Heroes (sic) and although it is very splendid to feel he has given his life for his country, the sorrow this news brings is overwhelming, and I hope and pray dear you may have strength given you to bear bravely this irreparable loss.

I wish I were able to help you to bear this great shock, but you have all my sympathy.

From Harold, a University friend serving with the South Wales Borderers, and equally oblivious to the difference between 'British' and 'English'!

I want to express my most sincere sympathy with you in the loss of your gallant brother, the news of whose death came so soon after the acknowledgment of his ability and valour. I am not in the habit of saying much, but I think it must be a great source of consolation to you that in dying he has added one more to the long list of English heroes whose fame will be everlasting.

From her friend Gladys:

I can't tell you how awfully sorry I was to hear about your brother. I saw it in the paper too but I was hoping that it wasn't he. Poor old Nancy! I know how you must feel it because I know how fond you were of your brothers and how much they were to you but Nancy you must be awfully proud of him. He was so gloriously brave and died fighting so nobly, the death of a real hero. Everyone says that he deserved the VC and that had he lived he would have had it.

The issue of a possible Victoria Cross became a cause which Granddaddy pursued in later life.

From another army friend, Rob Goodall:

I have just heard from Lydia that your brother is reported killed. I hope that it is incorrect (as so many of the official reports have been).

Even should it be only too true, he lived and died a hero, small consolation doubtless, at present when there is room for nothing but grief in your heart, but later something to be proud of.

And from another friend, Lydia:

I have just returned from wiring you on receipt of your card. How my heart bleeds for you Nancy. Nothing would give me greater relief than to be with you now. I can't express my feelings properly on paper. Do not give up your hopes Nancy. Many times have deaths been reported falsely in the papers. Has a wire been received from the War Office? How I hope the report is a false one. Be consoled, Nancy darling, by the fact of his glorious career – prolonged fighting and distinctive bravery. What more could he do for his country, Nancy? His is a noble sacrifice, in any case. I can't write, I feel your anxiety too deeply.

Nancy's last letter to Tommy was returned to her, the envelope simply marked 'deceased'.

My dearest Tommy,

I haven't heard from you for quite a time. Why haven't you written? I suppose you have had very little time. As you see from the above address I am staying with our cousins in Manchester. We all congratulate you on receiving or going to receive the Military Cross. I am indeed proud of my soldier brother. I knew you would prove yourself a true Erskine, and you have done so. Ralph is out there too now. I do hope he keeps safe too as you have done. I have just written to him. I have been here for a week now. I was at Cheadle Staffordshire for three weeks staying with a college friend. It was great. I enjoyed it immensely. I am going home to Auchterarder in bonnie Scotland next Wednesday or thereabouts. My address there will be 88 High Street, Auchterarder, Scotland. Do write me as often as you can. I love hearing from you. I am going into town tomorrow to meet the sister of another officer who was in Aberystwyth – Mary Lee.

I don't think I really have any more to tell you about myself. Nothing very exciting has happened – at least nothing that would interest you. We are quite a crowd here tonight – Jimmy's girl Doris and her brother. He is a ripping player and is strumming away just now. I do wish you were here with us. Everyone sends his and her love to you and heaps from myself to my brave soldier brother.

Goodbye

Your wee sister

Nancy

Tommy was buried in the small military cemetery at Brandhoek, between Ypres and Poperinge.

A couple of months later, he was awarded a posthumous M.A. degree with first class honours by Glasgow University.

After the war, his grave was given a standard headstone by the Commonwealth War Graves Commission. It was headed:

CAPT THOMAS BARRIE ERSKINE M.C.
ARG' & SUTH'D HIGHLANDERS
AND GORDON HIGHLANDERS
20TH JULY 1915

The length of the inscription allowed at the bottom was limited to 66 characters by the Commonwealth War Graves Commission and this is what Granddaddy chose:

M.A. (HONS) POSTH. GLAS. UNIV.
SON O'MINE
CAPT. J. ERSKINE
GORDON HDRS. & R.A.F.

5

NANCY – AND JACK

As described earlier, Nancy had been adopted by her uncle and aunt, John and Mary Black. John's job as a water engineer took him to Kidderminster, then to Aberdare, where she enrolled in Aberdare High School. Nancy was clearly an intelligent and hard-working pupil. Her school reports contained comments such as 'Her excellent marks indicate the praiseworthy work she has done.' and 'Has a special gift for exams.' Her excellent exam results led to her acceptance for a place at Aberystwyth University – a very unusual achievement for a girl at that time.

Welsh universities took students at a younger age than English ones and in September 1913, at the age of 16, Nancy enrolled for a BA course in English and Philosophy. She took up residence in the girls' accommodation of Alexandra Hall on the sea front, and threw herself into her studies. The following year the war broke out, and in the spring of 1915 a detachment of the Cheshire Regiment was posted to Aberystwyth for training. The rules about mingling with members of the opposite sex at that time were quite restrictive, but we can be sure that youthful ingenuity found ways round the rules, and plenty of interaction took place. At any rate, in June 1915 Nancy met, and subsequently fell in love with, a handsome officer called Jack Lee.

Jack was then coming up to his 24th birthday, and was the eighth and youngest child of William and Isabella Lee. William Lee was a classic example of a rags-to-riches Victorian businessman. William's father, John Lee, lived just outside Bolton and worked as a whitster, or bleacher, in the primitive woollen industry which existed on the Western Pennines. William left home at 13 and went to work as an office boy in Manchester in the tailor's business of an uncle. He trained as a tailor but had business ambitions and in 1873, in partnership with a Macclesfield silk merchant called John Kay, he founded a wholesale clothier's business called Kay and Lee. A few years earlier William had married Isabella Bowes, the daughter of an Irishman from county Monaghan who had come to Manchester and worked as a market toll collector. William and Isabella had eight children – five sons and three daughters – over the following 20 years, Jack being the youngest. Kay and Lee prospered, moving into premises in the Ancoats district of Manchester, near the area which has now been redeveloped to build Manchester City's Etihad Stadium and the surrounding facilities. By the turn of the century the company employed over 300 people, and William had become a very wealthy man. In the 1880s they lived in a fine house called The Willows in the Weaste district, but they were subsequently able to build an even more splendid house called Arncliffe in Crumpsall, North Manchester. However, his successful business career took a toll on William's health and, after a long period of heart trouble, he died in 1904 aged only 56.

No longer needing to be so near the business, his widow Isabella relocated to Cheshire, buying a house called Woodside in the then small village of Wilmslow. Her older children Harry, Nellie, Sidney and Stanley were married by then so the household consisted of the younger four – Bert, Isabel, Mary and Jack. There were also two live-in maids – Emily and Eliza. Bert worked in the family business as its sales representative for North America, while Jack gained experience in the clothing industry, working at a mill called Hollins in Marple.

When the war broke out, Bert was in Canada on business, but he returned straight home and he and Jack enlisted in the Manchester Regiment in October 1914. With their background, both would have been offered commissions, but Bert preferred to remain in the ranks with his Manchester pals. However, Jack took the opportunity, and in January 1915 he was commissioned as a 2nd lieutenant in the 6th Battalion Cheshire Regiment. His unit was sent to Aberystwyth for training and this is how he met Nancy.

We do not know if it was love at first sight, but in a short time the couple were very close. Over the next two years Jack wrote literally hundreds of letters to Nancy, which she kept faithfully.

The first of these is written on 16 July 1915, only six weeks after they met. Nancy's university term had ended and she had gone to stay with her uncle John Erskine in Manchester. It is several pages long, here is the beginning.

> My own Darling,
>
> Have not received your letter yet, but am expecting it any minute and longing for it. I am starting this now dearest, as this afternoon Billy, Frankie Chataway and I are going for a motor run most likely to Towyn – we have ordered the Humber for 2.15 so should not have much chance of writing after lunch. Do you remember our last run in the Humber dearest? When just us two went to dear old Aberdovey, I never enjoyed a run so much as that my darling and would give anything if we were only doing the same thing this afternoon, it would be 'great'.
>
> Where do you think Billy and I went last night? To the dear old Grove! … Oh my dearest I did long for you

all the way through, every little spot reminded me of you and the perfect times we have had there and I was really sorry afterwards that I had gone as I did not intend to go there again until I was with you, only poor old Bill was so down-hearted and there really seemed nowhere else to go. I wonder if you and I will be able to go to the old spot Nancy dear before the summer is over?

I was awfully delighted to get the photo and love looking at it, but dearest it is not half nice enough of you and I do hope that very soon you will really have a good one taken.

Clearly it had not taken long for Cupid's arrows to strike home. Only a few days later, Jack learned about Tommy's death.

It was a lovely surprise to have a letter from you this morning, as I hardly expected one, very many thanks for writing. I am more greaved *(sic)* than I can say to hear that yesterday's sad news is really true and I know how heart-broken you must feel. I know how hard it must be for you but you must do your best for the sake of your father who must feel this loss more than anyone can picture. I shall pray for you all my dearest in your great sorrow and I am sure that God will give you all strength to bear this loss.

I shall be thinking of you on your way to Scotland, what a sad journey it is for you.

A couple of weeks later:

My own darling girl,

Have just received your letter posted 2.45 pm yesterday, very many thanks for it – the posts do seem up the pole and as far as I can see it takes a day and a half to get a letter from you. *(They should be so lucky. RL)* I have got a bit of news for you – I am leaving here on Friday for a 3 week course in bayonet fighting etc at Newport – am really glad … as it will be a nice change from parade here. …

A week later from the Western Cavalry Depot in Newport:

Thanks ever so for your topping letter received this morning, along with five others, one each from Noel, Isabel, Mary, Rob and Billy Lees. I felt quite important getting such a post. Isabel tells me in her letter that you have written her. She thinks you are such a brick to have started this fruit picking and so do I as there is nothing like having plenty to do to keep one from getting depressed.

We haven't always relied on East European labour to pick our fruit.

At the beginning of August, Jack's older brother Bert had sailed for Gallipoli with his Manchester Regiment battalion. On 13 August a troopship carrying 1367 men from Avonmouth to Lemnos was torpedoed and sunk in the Aegean with a loss of 867 lives. The Lee family was naturally very worried.

I had a letter from Isabel this morning saying that my brother was not on the *Royal Edward*. Oh, Nancy you don't know what a relief it was, as since Monday I have been thinking all sorts of things and I could not make out why I had no letter from home, they were really upset at home when they saw the account, as the name of the boat had been censored in the letter they had from my brother, so they had two wretched days.

7 September was Nancy's 18th birthday.

> It has been a perfect day here and when I wakened this morning at 6.15 am I thought of you dearest and wondered how you were spending your 18th birthday. I do hope you've had a real jolly day my darling … you know all my love is yours.
>
>   Your own Jack x

Later that month there was some camp entertainment.

> The sergeants gave us a topping concert in their mess last night, it started soon after 8 and it was getting on for 12 before we finished. Sparkes, one of our new officers, sang about four times, he really has the most perfect voice and sang some topping songs.

In November Jack moved again – to the Artists' Rifles School of Instruction in Loughton, Essex.

> Here I am in the most awful hole you could wish to see. I left Oswestry on the 12.40 yesterday, got to London about 5 o'clock, went to a show at the Palace and came along here on the 11 pm. We are 2 miles from a railway station, in the middle of Epping Forest, we are billeted in empty sheds which I should think cattle have been kept in. The course starts in the morning at 7 am to 8 am, then 9 to 4.30, we take our own midday ration with us every day and have a lecture each evening from 8 to 9, no leave is being granted at all and we are not even allowed into Loughton which is 2 miles away. The only good thing dearest is the course is only 4 weeks but I bet it feels more like 4 months in this rotten hole.

We have no orderlies here and have to do all our own cleaning, such as buttons, boots etc but I won't bother you with all my troubles. …

A tough life! And in the early days of aerial warfare:

Very few lights are allowed here on account of raids. The Zepps have passed over here each time there has been a raid on London and I believe they are expecting another before the 11th so we may have some excitement before long. Two aeroplanes have been flying round all day and it has been very interesting watching.

December found Jack back in Oswestry.

I believe that there is just a chance of our being moved from here, as the camp is in such an awful state, you really have no idea what it is like – we cannot use the parade ground at all and the mud in the lines is quite 8 to 10 inches deep – it's quite impossible to get about, only in rubber high boots and then each step you take you nearly leave your boot behind you.

And the relationship was about to be put on a more permanent footing.

The CO asked me at lunch today how I had enjoyed Aberystwyth: wanted to know who I had seen and then finished by asking me if I was engaged. I told him no, simply because he's such an awful mess and I never felt inclined to tell him anything for one never knows how he will take it – if I'd said yes the chances are he would have said I should have asked his permission.

Christmas was approaching.

> No Xmas leave is being granted as we are giving the men a
> good Xmas dinner. The officers and sergeants are carving
> and waiting on them so it will be a pretty busy day.

Christmas Day in camp was busy.

> My own sweetheart,
>   Have only just finished midday dinner which we had
> at 3 o'clock, it is now 6.05 and the post goes at 6.15
> so have hardly a second ... We have had a very busy day
> here and shall have time tomorrow to write you a nice
> long cosy letter.
>   In haste, good night my beloved one.
>   All my love, your beloved Jack
> PS My leave has been granted for 3 Jan.

Though the family would not find out for several days, Christmas Day 1915 brought tragedy to the Lees. Jack's older brother Bert, serving with the Manchester Regiment in Gallipoli, was shot dead by a Turkish sniper. The tragedy was compounded by the fact that the ill-fated expedition was about to be abandoned, and his battalion pulled out three days later. He and a colleague from Droylsden called Leonard Hancock were the last two casualties in their unit.

Jack sealed their engagement by sending Nancy a ring, but the post let him down. He posted it on Christmas Eve, which was a Friday, but it wasn't delivered till the Sunday morning – Boxing Day. A contrast to today's Royal Mail service!

In January Jack enjoyed six days' leave and Nancy came to stay with the family in Wilmslow. When he returned to his unit, the prospect of being sent to France was emerging.

My very own darling,

Oh! I just feel too dark for words at the start of writing letters again sweetheart, for after six whole days with you darling it's going to be some job to try and settle down here again. ...

Burdett also informed me that he nearly wired for me last Wed to go to the 1st 6th *(Cheshire Regiment)*. He was very undecided whether to send Frankie or me, in the end tossed up for it and it fell to Frankie to go – so we were very lucky dearest to have had so long together. It seems the 1/6th went up to the firing line last Thursday and Sturton and Frankie along with two officers from the 2/6th sail from Southampton tomorrow. They both left here this morning. I don't know if this means that if any more officers are wanted I shall be sent, but it looks rather like it, but don't mention this at home darling for Mother will only worry. ...

I think I may be going on another course down at Aldershot pretty soon, for Bayonet Fighting and Physical Drill, as I saw the officer for this part of the training in the Battalion and since I took the course at Newport it's altered a bit, so this is a sort of refresher. I hope it comes off for I'm getting sick of this hole already.

In late January the news of Bert's death reached the family and Nancy wrote to Jack, prompting this reply:

Your beautiful letter full of love and sympathy arrived last night and I cannot tell you dearest what a comfort it has been to me – as you say sweetheart it is at a time like this almost more than any that our love for each other is of so much value ... I have stayed with Mother

and the girls and been able to brighten these dark hours
a little I think … To have seen Mother and how wonderful
she has been through it all, it does one good to hear her
beautiful thoughts and the beautiful way she looks at
dear old Bert having gone … Your letters to Mother and
the girls have been just beautiful and so comforting and
then those lovely flowers this morning were such a sweet
and kindly thought. We have had over 100 letters in the
last two days and everyone just writes the same about
dear old Bert and his beautiful nature and unselfishness
– for he just lived for others.

The journey to Aldershot was not without incident – Jack wrote
while waiting at Waterloo Station.

This is 'some' journey. I left Wilmslow on the 1.22, met
Arch in Manchester and we came up to London on the
2.10, had dinner and came to this station for the 9.10.
(Archibald Wood was Jack's brother-in-law, husband of
his sister Nell.) When we arrived we found no trains were
running and all lights out on account of a Zepp. raid – so
had to return to the Carlyle Club and phoned through
about 10 and found the trains were running again, so
the Zepps must have been scared off. Have now been
here about ½ hour and we are just starting off, shall
arrive at my rooms about midnight and expect I shall
find everyone in bed.

And the following day:

Have only just arrived here. As I told you in my note written
on the train, I did not get away from London till 10.40
and it was 12.50 when the train arrived in Aldershot.

These rooms are 4 miles from the station and as I had 2 bags and there were no cabs or taxis it was quite out of the question getting here. So I had to knock them up at a small hotel near the station. I then went on to the Barracks this morning – but as I had not been here could not very well come for lunch as I did not know how far it was away. So I had to walk into Aldershot which is 2 miles from Barracks – then after parade this afternoon I got a taxi, picked up my bags from the Ryl Hotel and came along here. I found the good lady of the home out, so managed to get the maid to make me some tea and had just finished when Mrs Harrison turned up. She seems quite decent but a typical Londoner. She has another old girl about 40 living here and as far as I can make out these are the only two people in the house. Mrs H has been out in France 12 months nursing and I think she said she expected a wounded Canadian officer in tomorrow.

In early February 1916 he wrote:

It's simply topping to hear that Ralph is in England and I do hope we shall manage to meet up in London … I think I mentioned in one of my other letters that there is a memorial service for dear old Bert on Sunday in Wilmslow and I feel I simply must be there and I know Mother will be awfully disappointed if I don't.

For some reason none of Jack's letters for the next three months have survived, so the story is resumed on 24 May when Jack was home on leave in Wilmslow and he received a telegram.

24/5/16 Report personally to Embarkation Commandant Southampton before 4 pm on the 26th

instant for orders stp acknowledge by wire
Commanding 6th Res Cheshire Regiment Oswestry.

So two days later Jack set off for France.

In the train 11.20 pm
My own darling sweetheart,
    Really on my way at last. I did not get a letter from
you yesterday dearest and felt sure there would be a
letter at camp and also one coming by this morning's
post. So I phoned the Postmaster at Wilmslow and
fixed up for him to send any letters for me down to
Woodside at 7 this morning – it was then sweetheart
that I got the two from my own little girl … *(Note
to Royal Mail: that's customer service. RL).* I left on
the 7.33, Arch came along with me, and then three
other boys and Eric met me at Stockport, where we all
left at 8.40. *(Eric was a nephew, son of Jack's oldest
brother Harry.)* Mrs Lees came down with Billy and
heaps of other relations down with the other chaps
and we had a fine send-off.
    Good bye my beloved and God bless you and keep
you safe for me. I feel that I shall be all the more worthy
of your love after having done my bit.
    With every little bit of my love darling.
    Your very own boy
    Jack xxxx

A few days later Jack arrived on the Western Front.

The post corporal may come in any minute but I just
want to send you a line dearest and will write you a long
letter later this evening.

We left Rouen on Monday at noon, got on the train at 4.30 pm and stayed on it till 12.30 pm yesterday, so had a nice little journey of 20 hours. This got us to a place about 6 miles from here, we then had to make our way to Divisional Head Quarters and in the end landed up here at 9.30 pm last night. The battalion had come out of the trenches the night before and I don't think will be going in again for a few days. We are about 3 miles from the firing line and one could hear the guns going all night. You'd laugh if you could see the place we are hanging out at – a little place that's been well shelled – there's not a window in the place and it all looks a wreck. Still it's better than nothing and I'm quite happy.

The battalion's initial position was near Givenchy. The following day:

We're really having a very slack time just now, only parading for about an hour each day ... but we are standing to and may have orders to move to the trenches any minute. ...

I was very surprised to hear that Ralph was out here again – if I do get a chance of seeing him, you can bet I shall. I have been made Company Bombing Officer, goodness knows why and I can see having a jolly time when we get in the trenches.

Given that Tommy had been killed doing the same job the previous year, I'm not sure what was jolly about it, but Jack's attitude was not untypical of the insouciant bravery of the time.

A few days later:

> We have just had orders that we are moving up to the
> trenches tomorrow. We go in supports for 4 days, firing
> line for 4 days, then back to supports and then back
> here.
>
> After tea yesterday, I had a long walk to a place
> about 4 miles from here, a little village that hasn't half
> been shelled, there's hardly a house standing, we could
> see the trenches quite clearly. I am delighted to say I
> am being transferred from A to C Company today and
> am really bucked as they are much nicer chaps in C.

A couple of weeks later Jack had his first experience of casualties.

> I was out with a working party and we must have been
> spotted for those damned Huns fairly gave us hell with
> machine gun fire and two of my men were hit. I can tell
> you that it was some job getting them in again and took
> us about an hour.

Parting from Nancy must have been an emotional event for
them both and around this time Nancy began to worry that they
may have said farewell too enthusiastically. She was concerned
she was pregnant. Jack told her to see a doctor and wrote several
letters full of guilt and remorse. He confided in his friend Billy
Lees, who recommended a very hot bath!

> 23 June
> There is a terrible strafe going on outside on 3 of our
> aeroplanes, it's awfully exciting to watch them dodge
> the old Bosch.

24 June

I was awfully sorry darling to hear about another cousin being killed. It really is a horribly sad case and awful for his poor wife. One only realises when out here how awful this war really is – to see villages in ruins and the poor French people, it makes your blood go cold. The house we are billeted in now is horribly knocked about, all the windows out and the roof smashed in and great holes in the walls. Yesterday morning an old old chap came around, about 90, and told us it was his home. You can see how nice it's been at one time and now just a wreck – one can't help getting dark at times out here sweetheart.

With the end of the University term, Nancy went back to the farm job she had had the previous year. Jack wrote:

Old Lizzie (the car) is no more. Arch has sold her for a van body to be put on and has bought a new car, painted blue and no end of a swank I believe. I hope we shall have a chance of sampling it. We got to our billets about 6 pm yesterday and they are not bad, we have two small canvas huts about 20' x 10', one for sleeping in and one for messing. The OC seems quite a decent sort of chap, he comes from Cheadle Hulme and knows Sid and Stan (Jack's older brothers) well. I can see such a lot of officers being wanted from the 3rd line before long – for such a lot of the old ones from here are going to the Flying Corps. We sent three yesterday and two more are expecting to go any day.

I hope you are going to have a real good month for although I'm sure it's going to be hard work on this farm, I'm quite sure you'll get plenty of fun out of it with there being six of you. Do get me a snap of yourself in trousers.

The first of July 1916 marked the opening of the ill-fated Somme offensive. Jack's 6th Battalion was stationed in the village of Richebourg St Vaast, a few miles to the north.

> I am awfully sorry to send you such scrappy notes the last few days – but it's been awful here sweetheart and some job to write at all – today we expected a big do coming off but it's been put off till tomorrow.
>
> (later) … It's very much quieter this morning as I sit writing this behind sandbags, one would hardly think the Bosch was only a few dozen yards away, or that there was any war at all. (7.15 pm) Have only just been able to get to this again dearest as from noon there's been a terrific bombardment.

A few days later Jack was still clinging to the hope that Nancy wasn't pregnant.

> I'm sure you would feel quite different by now sweetheart. Billy tells me that Kathleen feels quite different in fact did after a month, her back aches very much – does yours darling? I think I shall wire Arch and tell him everything – ask him how to get medical advice for you.
>
> In a letter from Mims (Jack's sister Mary) today she tells me that you're going to Woodside at the end of your month's work. I'm awfully glad sweetheart and only wish I could be there with you but I'm afraid Sept will be the earliest I can get leave. Arch has got his new car, which the girls say is 'it' so you will get some motoring in it no doubt.

At this time Jack's sisters Isabel and Mary were volunteering as nurses. Isabel wrote to Nancy:

Jack writes every day, I am thankful they are out of this 'push' *(the Somme offensive)* isn't it too awful, although we are doing so well, it is terrible to look at the casualty lists. Every hospital in Manchester is packed, and now I hear they are thinking of turning the Midland *(Hotel)* into one, but I don't think it can be true, it would cost such a tremendous lot to run it. We are very busy here, 10 stretcher cases came in last Sunday so we are kept on the trot, 10.00 in bed. I was working afternoons last week and today I am on from 1 to 7.30 as we are short-handed. Mims goes in the morning and now has to go at 7.30 instead of 8 as she has to see to the men's breakfasts.

In his next letter Jack confessed to a haircut and turned his thoughts to after the war.

I've not told you darling and perhaps it's a good thing I haven't – about 10 days ago I had every little bit of my hair cut off – you would never have liked me again if you could have seen me – I just looked like an Imp *(Imperial – presumably soldiers from the dominions such as Australia sported short haircuts)*, and the others hardly knew me.

How does Noel like the farm work? You'll know all about it dearest, if we take a farm when we are married won't you? It would be great to settle down to outdoor life when all this is over. I'm sure I could never start going down to Manchester again each day, although I had a letter from my old boss a few days ago saying he hoped it wouldn't be long before I was back again with him. If they'd make it say £400 a year one might consider it, eh sweetheart?

Jack turned 25 on 10 July 1916.

> I am back again with the battalion and hoping I shall have a letter from you tonight … This is a rum spot to be spending one's birthday in … Leave is stopped and goodness know when I shall see my own darling again. …

A week later:

> We came up to the trenches yesterday after all and have got quite a nice part of the line – at least it has been so far and I hope it keeps so. Have got rather a tiny dug-out but the men are building us a new one which will really be 'it' with room for a table and seat in it. The one Billy and I are in now – you have just room to crawl in and sleep nearly on top of one another.

And the next day:

> I've only time for just a few words. I've never had such a time as today in my whole life and I hope I shall never have to go through it again – have not had a wink of sleep since yesterday afternoon and our trenches have been shelled to blazes this afternoon so you can guess how I feel darling.

A week later Jack was out of the front line.

> I should think it was rather a nice change seeing everybody at the degree ceremony but can understand your being very glad to get back to the camp.
> It's jolly nice to be out of the front line for 6 days, as we had a very thick time – in fact the hottest time the

battalion has had since they came out in 1914. Now we are in support for 6 days, which is still in the trenches, but not so tiring. I'm writing this outside and the sun is simply pouring down and it's about the warmest day we've had this summer. I could just do with a dip from that slip in front of the Belle Vue darling and then a nice lazy afternoon on Constitution Hill with you.

And the following day, the ultimate luxury:

I haven't a scrap of news except that I've just had a hot bath this morning with my friend Wheatley-Jones. ...

30 July 1916

Phew! The heat. I just feel as though someone had dropped me in boiling water and it must be even worse for you darling working all day right under the sun – I don't know how you stick it.

    This new job as Transport Officer is tip-top and I feel no end of a nut at least I shall when I get my leggings and spurs. I had a topping ride last night from 6 to 7.30 with Frankie and my Sergeant. I was out for exercise with all the men at 6 am this morning for an hour. It's a great life and only hope I can keep at this job.

Just over a century ago the British Army was still on horseback! And the next day:

The heat is simply terrific here and I'm bitten all over my face and arms with the flys (sic). I look an awful mess. This morning we had a route march from 7.30 am to 11

am, it was terribly hot. and I was jolly glad of my horse
– which is really a beauty, black with white back feet. I
feel no end of a swank, especially now that I turn out in
spurs and a riding cane. With not doing any riding for so
long I am terribly stiff and sore, but expect it will soon
go off.

4 August 1916. The battalion had been withdrawn to rest billets
at Le Touret.

The battalion will be going into the trenches tomorrow
for a few days but I shall be staying here with the
Transport – expect we shall be on the move next week
early.

6 August 1916. A football match, an injury and a possible
engagement:

A football match was fixed between the officers and
sergeants and Billy was playing in it. I was watching with
Tubby and Ruddin and a few others – halfway through
Billy and another chap knocked into each other and
poor Billy was put out. The doctor went across and we
found that the poor chap had broken his ankle and was
in awful pain. We had to get stretcher bearers to take
him away and send for the ambulance. I stayed with him
all the time and after the doctor attended to him he
seemed more comfortable. I then saw him sail away in
a motor ambulance and I hardly think he will come out
here again – it will be 8 or 10 weeks before he can walk
and he's sure to get back to England pretty soon. He
was taken to a hospital about 4 miles away and I expect
will be there for a few days. I shall try and get down to

see him on my horse before he goes – I'm sorry he's gone for we've always been such great pals, but at the same time I'm glad he's safely out of it.

Have had a lovely long letter from Isabel and she mentions about Carl and Mary, it looks a sure thing they'll be engaged before long. I'm awfully glad for her – I'm very fond of Carl and I'm sure they'll be very happy, just as we shall be sweetheart when our time comes.

The officers beat the sergeants 4-1. There had also been a couple of cricket matches, married men v singles. The married men won both!

8 August 1916. Nancy saw a doctor and her condition was confirmed. Jack learned about it not from Nancy but from her friend Noel. He instantly agreed what they should do.

I was so hoping I'd have a letter from you today but I haven't – but I've had one from Noel written Friday. I hardly know what to say darling – all along I've been hoping against hope that it was not what we had thought, anyway now we know. ...

I've just written Arch a long letter telling him everything and giving him your address in case there's anything he can write you about. *(Jack's brother-in-law Arch, the Managing Director of Finnegan's department store in Wilmslow, had assumed the 'father figure' role in the family after William Lee's death.)* About getting leave sweetheart I'll do my very best but it will be an awful job – the battalion is in the trenches until Thursday – by then I shall have received the doctor's letter from Cheshire which I shall require to prove my case. Shall also have a long chat with Tubby – for it's awful not to have a pal to talk to now Billy has gone – then if I do get leave sweetheart, we'll get married by special licence. Oh, I do hope above everything else that I can get over dearest, for then I can make you my very own for always and always.

Have you had to tell your Auntie (Margaret) everything – I suppose you will, what a cur she will think me – oh Nance I'm not half good enough for you darling.

Goodbye my darling and remember I am always thinking of you and whatever happens I shall always be true to the one and only girl in the whole world that I love. Your own boy
Jack

9 August 1916. Still no letter, but news of Billy:

Darling I'm sure you know that if I could get to you at this minute I should but you've no idea how hard it is to get leave, and until I get the doctor's letter to prove my case I've not a chance of getting away.

I had a note from Billy this morning – he expected to sail for Blighty on Monday and he seems to be going along alright. He had his foot operated on last Saturday – he'll no doubt be in Blighty now. I'd give anything to change places with him, still no use wishing these days is it sweetheart?

After three days in the trenches, the battalion marched south to Villers-Brulin, where they stayed for nine days, undertaking various training exercises.

13 August 1916

What a rotter you will think me for not writing for three days dearest but really I haven't had a second. We have been on the march solid all the time, have halted in the evenings at 8 and then had to fix up places for the men to sleep and see the horses attended to and it's been 9 and after before I've sat down for a meal. About the three stiffest days I've had and I'm thankful to say that we hope to stop in this stop – it's a delightful little place, or at least it would be if I felt happy in my mind about you.

I'm writing in the garden of the chateau where we are billeted and it's just perfect –the most lovely old place with lots of cosy nooks, where we could have some lovely cosy talks.

14 August 1916

Tubby seemed to think the best place to be married would be Scotland – not near your home darling – but some town where I think one can get married much quicker than in England. *(Gretna Green, just across the Scottish border used to be a popular place to get married because Scottish marriage licensing regulations were less strict than those in England.)*

16 August 1916. An ultimatum from Arch:

Have only got time for a short note to let you know that I received the following wire from Arch this afternoon:

'Letters clearly show Nance's condition so desperate that it demands your immediate return for 2 days to meet her and myself in London. Explain the whole position to colonel and wire me in Abersoch'

I saw the CO this evening and my application will go on to the Brigade tomorrow, along with the doctor's letter and Arch's wire. I think I shall manage to get leave

in the course of a few days' time. I am going to wire Arch
tonight and ask him to arrange to meet you in London,
or come along with you to meet me as soon as I arrive.
I am enclosing a cheque to bring you along my darling.

Jack's application for emergency leave was granted and he
immediately travelled to London, where he met up with Arch.
Nancy and Granddaddy came south. On 24 August Jack and
Nancy were married by special licence in the church of St
James in Piccadilly. Sadly no photographs survive of this happy
occasion. The wedding party went to Daly's Theatre, just off
Leicester Square, to see a musical comedy called *The Happy Day*.
Jack and Nancy had time for a two-day honeymoon in Chester
before Jack had to return to his unit.

26 August 1916. On board the train to London Jack penned a
nine-page letter which began:

My own darling wife,
How glorious it sounds darling and to think you
really are mine always and always, how we've longed to
belong to each other for these last 12 months and now
we really do. ...
I felt I must do something as soon as I got on the
train and so I've been writing solid all the time and have
got through five letters and two postcards to the
family, thanking them for their wires and about keeping
the reason for our marriage just in the family and now
dearest just a few lines to you, although I can hardly
hold the pencil my fingers ache so. ...

Jack's sister Isabel kept a diary through these times which
recorded:

7 September 1916. Nancy's birthday (her 19th), all went to theatre to see 'A Little Bit of Fluff'. Mr Erskine came, met him in Midland and all came home together.

While Jack had been on leave for his wedding and brief honeymoon, his battalion had arrived on the Somme and were repeatedly in action near the German stronghold of Thiepval.

30 September 1916

It's glorious here today, the sun is pouring down. ...

I've just been reading Lloyd George's speech, my word darling it doesn't look like the war finishing this year, does it? You wouldn't think so either if you were over here although we are doing so splendidly. I was up on a hill this evening watching a fine British bombardment with the Adjutant. He said he'd been up earlier in the afternoon and with glasses could see one of our tanks at work quite easily. Lloyd George is right you know darling, it would be a crime to think of peace before we've really knocked the Bosch out.

The Cheshires were relieved on 4 October but returned to the front on 10 October. Jack's thoughts turned to the baby.

12 October 1916

The battalion are all in the trenches in a hot spot and don't think they'll have more than a few days and we're hoping to go back for a rest when they come out as they've had about 7 weeks of it and are fagged out.

I've just had an idea, I'll send you a list of names for our little somebody then you can let me know which you like or any others you know of … No dearest the list of names is no good – I started but somehow I want you with me, it's a job we want to be together for don't we.

Again the battalion was relieved for a few days before returning to the trenches. The weather worsened.

6 November 1916

I had to go out of the tent a minute ago and you're up to your knees in mud. It's enough to make a saint swear.

7 November 1916

I had letters from Mother, Mims and Mrs Beaumont (Norman's mother) last night. The latter has managed to get me 36 shirts and 56 pairs of socks for my men through the Stockport Comforts Fund.

In November the 6th Battalion was involved in a major action called the Battle of Ancre, the last major British action of the Somme offensive. After the battalion was relieved, it marched north to the Ypres salient in Belgium, where it remained until the ill-fated Passchendaele offensive over eight months later.

Christmas Day 1916

I was just settling down when the CO sent for me and it was 1.30 am before he'd finished his pow-wow. I was just about to settle off then when all the NCOs from the Coy came round and started singing carols in front of my dug-out so of course I had to invite them in for a smoke and it was about 2.30 before I settled off.

I can hardly realise it's Xmas day – we had a busy morning and I've been out this afternoon for 4 hours looking round the front lines. So of course it's just like every other day, except for letters and parcels.

Fancy dearest Feb 15 for our 'little somebody' why it will be here in no time – oh how glorious when it's all safely over and the wee darling has arrived.

27 December 1916

We shall be moving up into the front line in a couple of days, and it is a spot, water right over your knees, you can't knock about at all, only in high gumboots and we've 5 days to look forward to and then back here.

New Year's Eve 1916

Another 7 hours and 1916 will be over. What a year it has been for us two dearest, we've both had our sorrows and our joys but I don't think either of us has had any regrets, have we darling?

I've heard a whisper that the Sergeants are coming round at midnight to let the new year in, so I've got a bit of a spread ready for them.

6 January 1917

This waiting for leave gets harder and harder every day and you've no idea how sick I'm getting – things all moving so slowly – Morton goes today and so I'm hoping that the next may be mine.

8 January 1917. Promotion:

> I've got a bit of news for you which I'm sure you'll be bucked about. My captaincy came through last night and so that will mean more pay and will help towards our little somebody. 'Captain Lee' don't forget sweetheart when you address your letters.
>
> 11.10 pm – I've only just got in here. I feel tired out – am looking forward to a night's rest after 5 nights on a duckboard.

13 January 1917. A welcome parcel – nothing was too difficult for the postal service.

> Last night the gramophone which Mother sent me out for Xmas arrived – and so we had quite a gay evening. It really makes things quite jolly and when the war is over it will be fine for the nest.

14 January 1917

> Yesterday we moved from the line and today we've been settling down here. We've quite a good billet in a prison – we're here for a few days then I expect we shall move into the line again but I hear it's a better sector than the last one, not so wet. While we were here most of the men are on fatigues in the evenings – so tonight being our first where there aren't any, I fixed up a concert which has been quite a success.

With only two weeks till Nancy's due date, Jack's frustration naturally increased.

1 February 1917

Brierley lost his father and managed to get away on special leave today – I think ordinary leave will start again in a few days.

It's not been quite so cold today, we're still in camp – expect we shall move about Sunday to billets nearer the line.

3 February 1917

This waiting is so rotten it gets on one's nerves – it's making me as dark as old boots – I can't get to know anything about when I'll get away – Yorston finishes his leave tomorrow and he should be back Monday. …

I was awfully surprised to hear Ralph and Lennie were getting married in March – they've soon followed us, haven't they darling? Yes, it's a shame you can't go to the wedding.

4 February 1917

Quite a crowd of us had dinner out last night – The C.O., Major, Adjutant, Tubby, Spence, NEB and myself. During dinner the adjutant told me that I shall most likely be getting away in a few days – there's a leave for the 9th so at that rate I should be in Blighty next Friday … If I do come then it means I shall get to Wilmslow Friday night. I think the best thing to do is to have Saturday and Sunday at home and come to Carlisle Sunday midnight or Monday morning – I should then be with you till the following Saturday.

> We move from camp today to billets nearer the line
> and if I do get away it will be rather lucky, as I shall just
> miss a spell in the trenches.

Although now married, Jack still thought of Wilmslow as home.
Four days later his hopes appeared to be dashed.

8 February 1917

> I'm almost too fed up dearest to write. I never felt
> so dark in all my life – you'll just have got my letter
> of last Sunday, telling you I should be coming on leave
> tomorrow – I've not written since as each day I've been
> told everything was alright and that I should get away
> – and now just at the last moment I'm told that I can't
> – I'm to wait until we've done our next few days in the
> line – and I've actually got all my kit packed.

But it all came right in the end, though not without subterfuge
and a few dramas.

10 February 1917

On the train from Folkestone

> I sent you a wire before getting on the train dearest to
> say I really had landed … I'm nearly beside myself with joy
> at the thought of seeing my own sweetheart again – but
> oh! it has been a job darling to get here and every second
> I've been expecting to be stopped. I'll tell you why – after
> I'd written you on Thursday saying my leave was stopped
> again, I went down to my room and felt I should go mad
> – while I was there the Adjutant came in and I had a

long chat with him and he said he would do all he could to get me leave. Later in the evening he told me he had seen the CO and he had arranged for me to have leave from today. That meant leaving Ypres *(Jack can name the place as he's writing on the train in England and not subject to military censorship)* yesterday morning – I had ordered my horse for 10 am and was just finishing my packing when the Adjutant came in again with a wire from Brigade saying all leave was stopped. Well! You can imagine how I felt, just ready to come and stopped – the adjutant was awfully decent and said 'look here, you get away now and I'll show the C.O. the wire after you're gone.' I was off in two ticks, got down to the station 10 miles away and found that they knew down there about leave – this was about 11 am, the train leaves at 2.17 so I decided to risk it and got in the train with another chap out of the 29th Div. About 5 mins before the train started a sergeant came along to this chap with a note from his C.O. saying he had to rejoin his unit at once. I thought my turn next. The RTO *(Rail Travel Officer)* came along to examine warrants and said to me (I was in a carriage to myself) 'all divisions have stopped leave except the 39th but you'll be lucky to get through.' Anyhow I stayed on the train which didn't get into Boulogne until 2 am this morning, got a bed and went for the boat at 9 am, found it didn't sail before 11 am so had to wait about. Somehow I felt sure I'd never be allowed on the boat for the only people who seemed to be crossing were staff officers. However, I managed to get on without any questions being asked about my warrant and now dearest, I'm on my way to you. I should get to Wilmslow about 10 tonight and will wire you first thing in the morning what train I shall be coming to Carlisle on on Monday.

Jack spent the weekend with his family in Wilmslow then took the train north to see Nancy.

On the Monday Isabel recorded:

> Jack and I went to town and met Win. Lunch with Billy Lees and Karl. Jack went off to Carlisle on 12.35, all boys turned up.

His oldest brother wired Nancy to confirm:

> Just seen him off in splendour especially the boots that pinch happiest of times to you both Harry

12 February 1917. Jack's arrival in Carlisle, three days before Nancy's due date, will have been welcome on several counts. Nancy's maternal grandmother Margaret Barrie had died at the weekend aged 77, and her aunt Margaret Black had to return to Glasgow.

15 February 1917. Three days later, bang on cue, my father was born. Mary Lee, affectionately known as Mims, hastened to send her congratulations.

> My dears,
>
> What splendid news!
>
> I am so delighted for you both and especially to feel you are together! How proud you must both feel!
>
> We are wondering if Mrs Black returned from Glasgow and if nurse had arrived, we are most anxious for a letter, and expect you will have written us Jack.
>
> Of course I'm just longing to see the little darling, and will come to you Nance as soon as ever you want me. Isabel says she is coming first, very well! I'm at your service later.

Hope you received the wire of congratulations, sent off this morning, and that you will both get along swimmingly.

No time for more, in greatest haste.

Very much love to you both and kiss the darling.

Yours ever

Mims

17 February 1917. Only two days later, Jack headed south from Carlisle. He immediately wrote a 15-page letter which he arranged to have posted in Preston. It began:

In the train. 7.20 pm

The tears are running down my cheeks as I think of you both – I love you both so dearly and it is so hard to part with you – God only knows how hard. I spent the first half hour after the train had started with my eyes closed, dreaming of all the wonders of the last 6 days.

I've been going through all the names I can think of and I'm sure we couldn't think of a better one than – William Barrie Lee. How do you think it looks in writing dearest? Fine don't you think so? Oh, the wee pet – there never was such a perk of a baby.

Always your own boy,

Jack xxxx

Back in Wilmslow, Jack penned another 15 pages the next day.

I got into Exchange about 10.30. Carl met me but was too busy to take me home so ran me to London Rd and I got the 10.50 here. Mims and Harry met me at the station – he and Fannie had waited over here to see me

… Harry and Fannie were most excited about coming and of course the girls just dotty … This afternoon Billy Lees is coming over also some of the married ones and I'm leaving here on the 1.50 for London tomorrow with Sid and Arch and we're meeting Harvey for dinner. I should love to have met Ralph also but he's such a way out of town I hardly think there's a chance, but shall fix up his present today dearest.

The name darling everyone is charmed about and funnily enough Mother said she was sure that was the name we should fix on. William after Father and Bert, and Barrie after Tommy. So I'm awfully delighted.

Jack left the next day for London, from where he wrote again.

It has been quite a mess, found when we arrived last night no leave trains – and I heard this morning perhaps it would be Thursday before I could get away. However I've just been round to the station and hear trains are running tomorrow as usual so I'm nearly sure to get away then.

We had a nice little dinner last night with WM and Harvey – they both sent their love to you dearest, afterwards went round to the flat for ½ hour and met Mrs M. Today we were looking round – had a peep at 'our' church and the RAC for lunch. It did bring back our glorious little honeymoon. We saw Sid off on the 5.30 and Arch and I are going to a show tonight. He says he's sorry about Billy's name – he quite thought we should call him 'Bert Lee'.

And the following day (written on Grosvenor Hotel notepaper):

On the 7.50 am from London Wed 21/2/17

On my way at last … After I had finished my letter of last night, Arch and I went to 'Maid of the Mountains', it was produced in Manchester for Xmas and is a capital show. It's at Daly's and so of course reminded me of 'The Happy Day' *(the show he and Nancy had seen on their wedding night).* It was after 12 when we got in and with being up at 6 I can hardly keep my eyes open.

I don't quite know how I shall get along as regards this course – I'm due there at 3 pm this afternoon and the very earliest I can manage now is tomorrow afternoon. I wired the C.O. yesterday I might be two or three days late so perhaps he'll send Ruddin. I hope so. If the battalion are out for a month's rest then perhaps I'll manage a course just as they go in the line.

I don't want you to take any risks. I've been talking to Arch and he says you really should be on your back three weeks. If all goes well I daresay at the end of 10 days you'll be wanting to be up – well dearest just make up your mind to have an extra few days, it will be worth it. You want to remember what your poor little inside has gone through and three weeks rest just gives everything time to get back to its proper place.

When he finally reached the coast, Jack discovered that all sailings were cancelled due to the presence of German submarines in the English Channel. What do you do when you've got an unexpected day free? Go back to Carlisle of course! So Jack enjoyed the bonus of a few more hours with his wife and son. Tragically, it was to be the last time he would see them.

Heading south again, he wrote another letter from the train, which was posted at Carnforth – the station made famous by the film *Brief Encounter*.

In the train 8.30 pm

It's so hard parting with you sweetheart – now I just feel to be waking after a beautiful 2 days dream. Oh! It has been heaven darling, every moment bliss ... It's been so lovely to see the big change in our wee darling – he really is the sweetest thing that ever was. ...

I long for this rotten old war to finish, so we can be together for always and always.

And the following day en route to Folkestone:

Saturday 7.45 am.

I settled down directly after I posted my letter at Carnforth and slept nearly solid till 4.30 this morning, most of the time I had one side of the carriage to myself and so could lie down full length. The train got in at 5.20 and I managed to share a cab with another officer who I found out later was in Carlisle and had travelled on the 8.05 pm – an awfully nice fellow, a captain with the DSO, MC and South African ribbons – a regular. We went along to a YMCA place near Victoria and got a wash, shave and breakfast and now feel quite fresh again.

On arrival back in France:

> I got down to Folkestone at 10 am and on getting to the boat was told along with dozens of others to report at 2.30, so I had a walk round town with my Carlisle friend I told you about. We had a good walk along the front and then some lunch after which I wired you darling and then we made our way back to the boat. She didn't sail until * and it was * when we got here. I now find my train is 12.44 am. So I have got a nice long wait in this beastly hole … with dirty French people talking 20 to the dozen and making me feel sick of everything.

25 February 1917

> I'm writing this in Spence's billet and my word darling this has been a day of days for travelling. I got on the train about 12 last night and we were turned out at a little station miles from anywhere about 9.30, found our way to a Rest Camp, no one could tell us anything or where we should find the Battalion: it was about 6 miles from here so about 12.30 I left my pack etc at the camp and started off here – found a note from the Adjutant to say that my course was cancelled and that the battalion was in a camp about 3 miles away so I then had to clear off for my pack and have just got back here feeling fed to the world sweetheart. Spence has sent off for a cart and I should reach the Battalion about 9 pm with luck.

---

* Being sent from France, this letter was subject to censorship, and there are small holes in the paper where the boat times had been. Strangely, the censor didn't seem to mind about the train time.

Jenny Erskine with children (L to R) Margaret, Ralph and Tommy. 1896. Margaret died of meningitis a few months later.

The Great Britain boxing team which competed in New York. May 1911. Ralph Erskine is second from the right.

Tommy and Ralph Erskine in uniform

Tommy's death at Hooge Chateau July 1915, as illustrated in Great War magazine.

Granddaddy in uniform. Jack Lee and Nancy Erskine.

The wedding of Ralph Erskine and Lennie Higgins March 1917.

My parents' wedding in April 1941, with Barrie Erskine as best man. Fred Tattersall is just behind the bride, and behind him is Jim Nicoll, my mother's father.

Granddaddy, my father John Lee, his mother Nancy, and my uncle Ralph Tattersall.
Didsbury late 1940s.

27 February 1917

We left the camp that I found the battalion at early this morning and all just settling down in another one which isn't half as nice I'm sorry to say, don't know how long we're here for dearest but I'm hoping to be sent on a course within a week or two.

1 March 1917

This will be a very very tiny letter tonight sweetheart for I don't think I've ever been so tired – oh yes, a fortnight ago tonight darling when I went off in front of the fire. Six of us had to go to the trenches this morning – we left here about 9 am & didn't get back till 4 pm, on the go the whole time, I'm nearly dropping to sleep as I try to write.

There is a gap of a month till Jack's next surviving letter.

4 April 1917

The post was early today and I got your letter of Fri about 2.30 pm with the pc for which I've been living for days enclosed. Dearest it's beautiful – the wee perk, he looks a perfect angel and I could eat him, I just wish he was on your knee darling instead of nurse's – still I shall look forward to one of the two of you in a week or so, for Isabel has promised to get it done while she is with you.

Sidney and I have had a very nice afternoon out – we got bikes from the Orderly Room and cycled into the town – this wasn't anything special as the roads here are the last word. The great thing was we had a decent hot bath and I now feel I am a nice clean little fellow. …

We're moving from here tomorrow dearest and going right back for a rest, hope we get the same farmhouse we had before Xmas as it was quite a nice little place and very comfy for out here. How long we shall be resting I don't know. Still if it's only a couple of weeks it's better than none at all. It's quite a good march – about 16 miles from here, so we shall have to make an early start.

8 April 1917

What a perfect morning – the sun is shining through the window as I write and one feels more than ever what a wicked sin it is that this wicked war is raging and keeping us two apart when we might be out together with our darling boy. My word sweetheart the 'Brownie' (a Kodak box camera) would be busy this morning if I was at No 176 for the light is fine and I do hope Isabel isn't losing the chance of a few snaps.

Sidney and I intend to have a stroll this afternoon as there are no parades today with it being Sunday. I started this before dinner and then had to leave it as the Doctor turned up for lunch, he's been inoculating the whole Company.

For some reason only one letter survives from the next two months.

20 May 1917

III Corps School, BEF France
My very own darling little wife,
    I quite intended to write you yesterday afternoon, but it was so hot I got on my bed at 2 and didn't waken

again until after 4. We had a lecture at 5.30 and after that I went into town and met Yorston for dinner. The battalion are still in Camp so I'm going over to see them at 11 and spending the day with them.

2 June 1917

We arrived in camp about 6 pm last night all feeling about tired out for we had a long march about 18 miles and the heat was terrific. I found a topping mail waiting for me darling – long letters from Isabel, Nellie and your long one of last Sunday for which heaps of thanks precious.

I'm writing this outside but it's an awful job to get comfortable as, apart from the tents which were pitched yesterday, there's nothing in the camp at all, not even a box to sit on. I've not heard from Tubby since he went into hospital last Sunday – I wonder if he's on his way to Blighty * – lucky bounder. I think we shall be here 3 or 4 days on a big fatigue, then we go back again for training.

The battalion was now in billets near Poperinge and the men spent the next few days on fatigue duties, bringing up ammunition supplies for the Royal Artillery.

3 June 1917

There is a cricket match on this evening and a bit later on I shall get the old gramophone going.

Soldiers often reckoned a minor wound which led to being sent home was a good deal.

4 June 1917

It's 9.30 pm and I'm writing this outside – it's about the first time today I've been cool. It's really been a scorcher and it's now just perfect and I long to be with my own little girl and that perk of a boy more than ever. ...

The doctor heard from Tubby Brown's sister today – what do you think? He's in Whitworth St Hospital, Manchester – it's only 8 days since he was wounded so he must have got across in 3 or 4 days – isn't he just too lucky for words darling?

Jack was not being ironic here – see above.

5 June 1917

I've had a very busy day fixing up sports which we started at 5 pm and carried on until 9 pm and we finish them tomorrow. How is that perk of a boy? I'll bet he's as brown as a berrie (sic) with all this sun – I'm nearly black.

6 June 1917

I'm feeling rather dark tonight sweetheart – for one thing the rain has started and the other is that I haven't had a letter from you dearest ... As regards news I really haven't a scrap darling – all the battalion have been out loading shells – you've no idea what the artillery has been like round here for the last few days – just like one long earthquake – of course we're well behind the line – it must be pretty awful in it.

I had a letter from Stan (Jack's brother) today – quite an event for he hates writing. They've been down at Rhos-on-Sea for Whitsun, then going into another house in a week or two – nearer Bramhall Park.

8 June 1917

The band is playing outside my tent and it's a glorious summer evening. ...

12 June 1917

We had such a topping billet last night we decided to have a bit of a burst and so it was getting towards midnight before I turned in. I had to be up at 4 am and we paraded at 5.50 and marched until 3.30 pm with just an hour's rest at 10 am – so you can guess I feel pretty weary tonight darling – the men have really stuck it fine as the heat has been awful for marching – we're off again in the morning but only have about 6 miles or so further to go.

I'm writing this at my bedroom window which is in the farm – where all the men are billeted in the barns. Most of them have turned in as they're about fagged out. We arrive in the training area tomorrow and I hope will be there for a week or two.

The training area was at Coulomby in France, a march of about 40 miles.

14 June 1917

I'm sorry I missed writing yesterday darling but I hadn't a second and today has been the same and now it's 10.50 pm and so I'm afraid this will be a very short letter as I've to be up at 6 am – we're very busy training and one hasn't a minute. Sunday we have off so shall hope to write a long letter then.

15 June 1917

I'm so busy I hardly know where to turn. We left here at 8.30 this morning for the training area and it was after 4 when we got back. …

I also had a long letter from Mims just full of Billy – she says she has never seen such a fine babe for 4 months and that he's just perfect – she's longing to have you at Woodside so that you can show Billy off. Fancy that the perk is 4 months old today, how time flies.

17 June 1917

I've hardly had a minute – Sunday to Wed we were on the march and since then we've been at it hard training until today which we had off – except for church parade this am, when we had a drum head service * which was very nice and reminded me of Oswestry.

19 June 1917

I was sorry to miss writing yesterday sweetheart, but we were out from 8 am to 4 pm and then I'd a heap of things to do but really felt too tired to write so please forgive me – today has been nearly as bad – we started off at 7 am and it was 6 pm before we

---

* The stacking up of the drums is an Army tradition, the drums, long ago, being piled up to form an altar whilst the Army was in the field.

got in, so it has been a jolly full day and I feel about tired out ... We're moving from here again the day after tomorrow to another training area for a week or two I expect. Yes the air raid on London really is awful, as you say one doesn't seem safe anywhere these days.

You say you are writing in the drawing-room with the perk by your side on a cushion and I can just picture you both dearest and it makes me ache to be with you – he really must get sweeter every day – I love his little trick of blowing bubbles out of his tongue.

20 June 1917.

We've finished a little earlier today and were back in billets by 2.30 pm – it's quite a treat and about the first afternoon I've had to myself since we came here. We are moving from here tomorrow to another training area for about 10 days or so – it's about a 15 mile march.

The weather seems to have quite broken today and we keep having awful thunderstorms – luckily we've been under cover for most of them so far.

21 June 1917. Jack sent a postcard with a photo of St Omer.

Am sorry have only time for a pc, have been on the march nearly all day and am just getting settled in fresh billets which are quite nice – no mail today so hope for a letter tomorrow. Heaps of luck. Jack.

This march took them to Moulle, ten miles to the north-east.

22 June 1917

There have not been any parades today, with our only arriving yesterday and the men have been able to clean themselves up. It's been an awful day – rain, rain, rain – quite a change after all the heat. All the officers had to go at 1 pm to look at the new training area, which is about 5 miles off. I went on my gee, got back about 4 pm soaked to the skin. We start training again tomorrow – parade 7.30 am so I intend to get to bed early tonight. …

I was very glad you were going to Mrs Storey's last Mon – as you say dearest it would be a nice change. …

I'd give worlds just to have a peep at Billy for I feel to be missing such heaps of his perky ways and it's so lovely to hear that his hair is curly and that he's got such blue, blue eyes.

28/29 June 1917

We're leaving here tomorrow so I'm standing the Company a bit of a do tonight then on the 2nd I go on a course for four days – three other company commanders are going from the battalion so it should be a rather nice change.

Fri 29th

I hadn't time to finish this last night sweetheart and have only a few mins before post time – I was just expecting to go on the course this morning when it was cancelled and so I'm now in camp with the battalion and expect we shall go in the line in a day or so.

30 June 1917. After their period of training for the forthcoming assault on Passchendaele, the battalion went back into action,

returning to the hilltop sector near Wieltje, just to the north-east of Ypres.

> Phew! What a day, it's raining for all it's worth and has been doing since first thing this morning and to make me feel bright and cheerful we go in the line this evening – it won't half be a picnic still we mustn't grumble, for we've had a good spell out, especially me, I don't think I've been in the line since the end of April.
>
> I had to go up the line after arriving last night and it was 5 am this morning before I got back to bed so I think I'll try and manage a few minutes shut-eye this afternoon.
>
> How's Ralph these days dearest, do you ever hear anything of him? Three Officers from this battalion have gone to the Flying Corps this week – I think I'll transfer, perhaps there'd be a chance of a few days in Blighty.

Jack was chosen to command a daring raid on enemy trenches which took place on the night of 4/5 July.

This description is taken from 6th *Battalion the Cheshire Regiment in the Great War* by John Hartley.

> Almost immediately plans were made for a raid on the trenches opposite, Caliban Trench and Caliban Support Trench, to be led by Captain Jack Lee.
>
> Captain Lee commanded a party of three officers and 133 other ranks, including several Royal Engineers. The raid was planned to take place in the early hours of 5 July. Three days prior to this, Lee and his men were withdrawn from the front line so they could practise the attack on a full-size mock-up of the area. It meant that every man knew what was expected

of him. The objectives of the attack were detailed in the battalion war diary:

'Killing or capturing as many of the enemy as possible; capturing and destroying war material; destroying dugouts, machine guns, trench mortars, dumps, tramways etc; gaining information regarding the enemy's front line system and troops occupying same; to lower the morale of the enemy.'

The preparatory work for the raid was carried out meticulously. Gaps were made in the outer bands of the German defences by a combination of British artillery fire and men going out into No Man's Land with wire-cutters. During the evening of 4 July gaps were cut in the inner bands of wire and, shortly before the time of the raid, a reconnaissance patrol of one officer and five men went out to check there was still a way through. They were able to confirm that a five-yard path had been made and that marking tapes laid out the night before were intact and the raiders only had to follow these to the gaps. There was also a ruse to distract the Germans. The units to the left of the Cheshires co-operated by arranging a feint attack. British artillery and machine gun fire would play on their part of No Man's Land and, when the time came for the raid, their soldiers would raise dummies, intended to indicate that a raid was under way there. It was hoped that it would distract the Germans sufficiently to allow the Cheshires to get into the enemy trench.

4 July 1917. Just before the raid, Jack wrote a brief note.

You can rest assured sweetheart if there was a possible chance of getting any leave I should but it's stopped with a big 'S'.

I'm going into the line tonight again – and shall do my best to write to you in a day or two, but you know how busy I am when in the line dearest.

From 6th *Battalion the Cheshire Regiment in the Great War* again:

Zero hour was set for 2 am. Five minutes before this, the Cheshires' scouts spotted an enemy patrol about 30 yards away in No Man's Land. The Germans opened fire on the scouts and fire was returned, at which the Germans started to retire back to their own trench. However, before they could reach it, the planned British artillery barrage opened up, cutting off their escape. Four or five of them managed to get away but the others were killed by the barrage or by the raiders when they reached them. Company Sergeant Major Arthur Shackley bayoneted several of them. Shortly after, the Cheshires were in the enemy trench, where they came across a group of about fifteen Germans who were attacked and killed, with the exception of four men, three of them wounded, who were captured and taken back to the British lines. As they advanced through the trench system, more German defenders were accounted for and another three captured.

Meanwhile the Royal Engineers sappers were placing charges but only two small dugouts were demolished, the larger ones being constructed from concrete and too strong for the charges available. Thirty-five minutes after zero hour, Captain Lee ordered the withdrawal back to the British trench.

The entire raid had gone to plan. A German officer had been killed and all his papers and maps were brought back and handed over to Intelligence Department. Seven prisoners were captured. Five were wounded and the official report on the raid notes that all of these 'expired on the way to our trenches'. The other two men and their escort had a lucky escape as they were buried by a shell explosion. British casualties were very light, with only two men being badly wounded. However Lieutenant Denis Crew was posted as missing, believed killed.

The battalion diary noted:

> The raid was a great success and earned much credit for the Battalion and its C.O. Colonel W H Stanway, DSO, MC and Captain J Lee, who commanded the riding party. Every man knew his task thoroughly and the enemy trenches by heart. It was quite a model raid, and secured valuable information.

> Two Military Crosses and four Military Medals were awarded.

One of the Military Cross awards was to Jack. The citation read:

> For conspicuous gallantry and devotion to duty when commanding a raid. His conduct throughout was of the highest order and a splendid example to the men. It was entirely due to his fine leadership that the enterprise was successfully carried out.

Jack wrote to tell Nancy of the raid.

> I feel jolly thankful to be here and able to write to my own little sweetheart – for as you will hear in the letter I've sent home, I made a raid on the Bosch last night with my company and of course I've not mentioned it in any of my letters to you dearest because I knew you'd only

worry and when I wrote you yesterday before going up the line I couldn't help wondering what my fate would be – but God has been good to us darling and I'm thankful to say I came through without a scratch and the whole thing was a fine success. The only rotten part is one of my officers (Crew) is missing and believed killed – still I've not given up hope yet and perhaps he may turn up tonight when it gets dark.

There are heaps of things I should like to tell you dearest – but shall have to leave it until we meet. I'm off at 7.30 am in the morning on 14 days rest down on the coast – of course it will be a jolly nice change and I'm jolly lucky to be missing another 11 days in the line. Still I only wish it was 10 days in dear old Blighty with my own little sweetheart.

After his nocturnal heroics, Jack was granted some well-earned rest at the French coast.

8 July 1917

I'm sorry I couldn't manage a letter yesterday sweetheart but I was travelling all day, got on the train at 7.30 am and it was 6 pm before we reached this camp. It's a delightful place right on the cliffs overlooking the sea – about 4 miles out of town. I'm writing this on the cliffs dearest with my face towards dear old Blighty and if it was only clear I should be able to see the coast quite clearly – but it's terribly hot and there's a thick sea mist – it's just perfect here darling and I'd give anything if you were only here with me. It's so delightfully peaceful only just a few farms and fishermen's cottages scattered about and then all the tents, which as long as the weather holds are top hole.

I'm sorry to say that up to leaving yesterday morning, nothing had been heard of Crew, the officer who was missing after the raid and I'm afraid he must have been killed – it really is rotten luck, for apart from that I only had 4 light casualties in the Coy. Perhaps I shall hear something in a day or two.

When is Billy being christened dearest? Now Elsie's boy's been done – perhaps you'll have it done this weekend while Auntie is with you.

Sadly, Jack's fears about Lt Crew were correct.

Lieutenant Dennis Crew was a 22-year-old silk finisher from Macclesfield. He had been bayoneted and the raiders assumed he was dead. Still alive, he was captured by the Germans and evacuated to a field hospital, but died soon after arrival. After he was reported missing, his identity disc was returned from Germany; he had been buried by the Germans in Westroosebeke Communal Cemetery, and as his grave was later destroyed, he is commemorated by a special memorial.

9 July 1917

It's rotten here today – a cold wind and drizzling with rain.

After writing yesterday I walked into town – it just takes an hour and 10 mins – had a look round then dropped across a couple of chaps I know so we had dinner together and I got back just after 10 pm. The other officer who shares this tent with me is only a youngster and rather a fool – anyhow he wants me to go into the town with him, so I think I will as there's nothing to do here it being so wet – quite impossible to go and sit down on the shore.

What an awful air-raid over London. One of the chaps I had dinner with last night had crossed yesterday morning and seen it all – he lives just outside. They seem to do more damage with planes than they did with Zepps.

10 July 1917

5th Army Rest Camp, APO S31, BEF, France

My very own darling little wife,

It's a heavenly evening sweetheart and I'm writing this outside my tent looking across the Channel – the sea is as calm as a millpond and one can just see Blighty. My word I'd give something to just be crossing. Have had quite a nice day dearest. I started off at 11 am with two other chaps and we walked to a little place about 4 miles along the coast. In peace time it must have been a great holiday place for there are some topping houses but now they are all in use by the Red X and there are heaps of wounded knocking about, it's an ideal spot for them. We had lunch at this little spot and then an hour's shuteye then got the tram into town, had a look round and then walked back here in time for dinner at 8 pm.

With it being my birthday today – 26, I'm feeling quite old darling and wonder if you happen to have thought of 2 years today since we had the afternoon and evening together in Stoke – my word that was a great day wasn't it? I just had the weekend off from Aber to see old Bert as he was on his last leave.

Tell the girls it was this place that Bert Summerset (a friend of the Higgins and Hornabrooks) came over to build a house for the Duke of something or other before

the war – of course it's not a bit like the p/cs now –
heaps of houses closed up – not a soul on the shore or
prom except wounded Tommies. Still a delightful spot.

Jack also sent his mother a picture postcard. It was of Hardelot-
Plage, a small resort between Boulogne and Le Touquet.

The country here is perfect – as you can judge from
this pc. Nance will give you all the news from my letters,
expect I shall get some letters any day now forwarded
from the battalion. Have had quite a nice birthday –
only hope I'm home long before my next.

Best love to all. Jack

12 July 1917. Jack sent Nancy a postcard showing a smart
restaurant called *Le Pre Catalan*.

Had dinner at this delightful spot last night with three
other chaps reminded me very much of Aberdovey – no
letter from you yet dear – hope there will be one today.
The weather is just perfect here and I hope it's the
same with you.

Will write later – heaps of love to you both. Jack.

And later a letter:

The weather is just perfect down here and I'm quite
enjoying this change – as I told you on the p/c I sent
this morning I had dinner out last night with 3 officers
from the artillery – we left about 5.30 pm just intending
to stroll down the coast for a bathe – then the time got

to 7 pm so we decided to dine out – one of them knew the spot I sent you the pc of and it really is the most perfect garden – glorious trees all round a fine lawn where we had dinner under the trees and the flowers were glorious, roses by the hundred – it just reminded me of some spot in Blighty and oh sweetheart how I longed for you. I thought of the perfect talks we could have had under the trees and the cosy times after dinner. We got into conversation with 4 Yanks*, doctors, and it was 11 pm before we started back and getting on for 1 am when I got to bed.

Today I've been into town, bought a new cap as my own was quite done and also had a hot bath and came back here for dinner. It has been a perfect day dearest – about the warmest we've had and so you can guess the night it is – if I was only at Woodside I could see us both taking a stroll down the lane towards the Carrs before turning into a cosy bed for a very cosy night.

I've been expecting a letter daily from the battalion about Crew the boy who 'went over' with me a week ago and was reported missing believed killed – for until I know something definite I can't write his people – his father is the Mayor of Macclesfield.

I leave here on the 20th a week tomorrow. Please thank Mother very much for the parcel of cake, butter and sardines which arrived today and tell her I'll write in a day or two.

God bless you both and keep you safe and well for
Your own own boy
Jack xxxxx and x for the perk.

---

*The USA had entered the war in April and US troops were just starting to arrive in Europe.

13 July 1917

I am glad you got the letter with the copies of the wires enclosed – am sorry to say nothing more has been heard of Crew – it really is black and I'm going to write his people tonight, a most awkward letter to write for I can tell them so little about the affair – when I get leave I shall try and slip over to see them – of course he may have been wounded and taken prisoner – but I'm afraid he was killed.

There's a large YMCA in connection with this Rest Camp and the 4 girls who help there – I call them girls but two are quite old dames – seemed quite good sorts although I didn't speak to them.

Many thanks sweetheart for your congrats on the little show – it was a great success except for Crew and that's worried me awfully.

It's a perfect evening and just going dark 9.40 pm. I'd just love a stroll along the cliffs here with my little wife so I could tell you some of the things I want to but can't put in a letter.

14 July 1917

It's been a very slack day. I got rather an exciting book from the YMCA last night – a proper blood – and as it was very showery spent the whole morning on my bed reading, and the same until 4 pm this afternoon when I finished it.

15 July 1917

I've only had one letter today and that's from Sydney.

They are all out of the line now and are jolly thankful as they've had a rotten time.

I went down to the town at 9.30 this morning as I got word last night that two officers from the battalion were down there on their way to the Flying Corps – so slipped down as I wanted to get the latest news of the battalion – had lunch, saw them off on the train and then spent the afternoon on the sands reading – the band was playing on the prom and it was a nice change. I got back here about 7 and have just finished supper. It's been another perfect day.

17 July 1917

It's a perfect evening – or at least it would be if you were here dearest – there's not a ripple on the sea and I'm sure one could cross to Blighty in a canoe.

There's nothing to do in town and one gets rather bored. I managed to get my hair cut and when I was paying, the man (a Frenchman) slipped a small box in my hand with the remark that 'there's a really good show on at the theatre this afternoon with lots of nice girls'. Needless to say I didn't go.

Jack went on with an embarrassed description of the contents – condoms.

19 July 1917

Officers Club

I couldn't write last night as there was a most awful
storm – wind and rain – I thought the camp would be
blown away and it was impossible to keep a candle
in.

I had a very big mail yesterday – 6 letters – yours,
Nellie, Marjorie, Mims, Geoff Bowers and one from
Rowley of C Company am sorry to say his contained
some rotten news – the night they were coming out
of the trenches, Brierley (Duckboard Bill who sent you
the little cap for Billy) was hit by a shell and killed on
the spot – it is rotten luck – he has been buried in the
same little cemetery that Tommie *(Erskine)* is in at
Brandhoek, between Poperinge and Ypres.

Let me know what you think of the houses round
Styal darling. My word it would be heavenly if we were
just picking our own little nest, wouldn't it?

Our train doesn't go till 2 pm but we have to be at
the station at 1 and I expect it will be getting towards
9 or 10 before we get off so I don't suppose I shall find
the Battalion tonight.

So Jack's leave came to an end. It's comforting to
know that he enjoyed a relaxing break in view of what
was to follow. The following day he had a proud moment.

20 July 1917

I'm sorry I couldn't write last night sweetheart but it
was 10 pm before I reached the Batt after all day on the
train and 1 am before I got to bed.

Today we had a busy day training from 7.30 am to 4 pm – were in billets and all quite comfy at 5.30 pm.

I received the enclosed wire – which please keep for me – I know you'll be pleased to hear I've got the M.C. sweetheart and I wish you could all have been here this evening. The battalion were formed up on 3 sides of a square while the General addressed them about C Company and the raid. I must say I felt very proud and I think I can say dearest one of the proudest moments of my life (except when you became my own little wife and that darling Billy arrived) was when the General pinned the ribbon on my coat. This I'm going to send home in a few days when I've had some other ribbon pinned on. I'm awfully glad that Rowley also got the M.C. and I got the DCM for 2 other NCOs and the MM (Military Medal). So we've done jolly well.

Just in case you don't happen to know darling when addressing letters to me now you put 'M.C.' after my name. (Swank!)

The wire read:

In confirmation of this office wire No A810 stating that 2/Lt (A/Capt) J. Lee 1/6th Bn Cheshire Regt has been awarded the Military Cross by the Field Marshall Commander-in-Chief. The enclosed medal is forwarded for transmission to the recipient of the medal.

Please convey the Divisional Commander's congratulations.

(Signature illegible) Lieut-Colonel.

AA & QMG 39th Division.

Two days later the battalion marched to Moulle and then moved by motor bus to St Jan Bitzen, to the west of Poperinge.

23 July 1917

I'm so sorry dearest I didn't manage a letter yesterday but it was quite impossible – we were on the move all day and it was 2 am this morning before we got into this camp. As I said in my last darling my letters will be short and few this week or so as we've a heap of work to do.

I had a letter from Billy Lees today – he's just got another 2 months light duty – lucky dog.

I'm enclosing the medal ribbon I told you about sweetheart – which I know you'll be glad to have as a little reminder of July the 5th.

Mother said you had been for a drive round Styal and that you quite like the place darling and would like to live there – so would I – anywhere as long as I have you.

25 July 1917

Phew! What a day it's raining like blazers (sic!) and I'm trying to keep dry in a tent that's been patched in a good many places and there are already 3 little ponds around my feet. I'm awfully sorry sweetheart that I couldn't manage a letter yesterday but had to clear off on my horse with 3 of the others at 11 am and it was 7.30 pm before we got back – dog tired. It was a very close day and gave me rather a rotten head, so I just couldn't write.

The Army was still using horses as it prepared for the Passchendaele offensive.

On the same day Nancy wrote to Jack to congratulate him – a letter which he never received and which was subsequently returned to her.

Darling Boy o'mine,

I don't know what to say to you. I am so proud of you. Fancy you getting the M.C. I simply can't tell you in words darling what I think of you but when I see you next I shall be able to show you. Of course I'm not a bit surprised – I knew you'd do something fine. We were so excited this morning (mother and I) that we couldn't eat our breakfast. Mother rang up everyone to tell them the news and we were just like a pair of lunatics. I told Baby all about it but he just roared in my face – as much as to say 'you dotty loo'. And that's just what I feel today. I could scream with pride, you dear old darling thing. The point is does it mean a bit of leave cos it ought to and I feel I must see you now. I expect you're two inches taller. And you're so modest about it all, but I'm not I can tell you darling.

I'm too excited to write, I'll write again tonight when I'm calmer, so I'll ring off now.

Goodbye my own M.C. you're the finest soldier in the world.

All my love to you dearest,
Your own little wife
Nance xxxxx
X Billy

26 July 1917

Have had a very busy day – cleared off in a motor bus at 10 this morning to go and look at some trenches and it was 4 this afternoon before I got back. Last night we had a very jolly evening – the CO stood all the officers dinner at a little place about half an hour's walk away. We did expect to move from here today but now it's been cancelled.

28 July 1917. The Passchendaele offensive was imminent.

I think we shall move from here in the morning dearest – to another camp – and am not sure if I'll be able to manage a letter tomorrow, I will the following day. Then I'm afraid it will be 5 or 6 days before I write again as we shall be terribly busy in the line – so don't worry darling, you may rest assured that I shall write to you the first chance I have darling.

I've just had an officer from the Brigade in to see me and it seems 'my raid' was the largest and most successful that has been done in the Division since they came out – so this is rather pleasing.

29 July 1917

I'm so excited at reading your letter with the snaps enclosed that I hardly know how to write – never, never, never have I seen such a perk – he just looks as though he would jump off the photo as I look at him and make one of those sweet little noises you've told me about dearest. Oh! He really is heavenly and I couldn't help tears coming into my eyes as I read your sweet letter dearest and looked at the snaps. The 'wanting feeling' was so awful. ...

We made an early start this morning, left camp at 6.30 and arrived here about 9 – just before the rain started and it was a good job we got in before as it poured all day.

The battalion had marched to Elverdinghe, about 4 kilometres north-west of Ypres.

30 July 1917. The battalion diary recorded that they moved at 8.35 pm to take up position in 'X' line at La Brique, prior to the forthcoming attack.

Jack wrote what was to prove his final letter.

> The weather is pretty rotten again today, wet all morning but cleared a bit this afternoon.
>
> Oh my precious how I adore you. You're the dearest little wife in the whole world and I'm going dotty for a glimpse of you sweetheart.
>
> Now my beloved – I'll have to stop as I'm an hour behind my time for shut-eye already – shall do my best to write you again in 4 or 5 days – so don't expect a letter before sweetheart.
>
> All my love to my own little girl – the best little wife in the whole world and a great kiss for Billy Bubbles.
>
> God bless you dearest and keep you safe and well.
>
> Your own Jack xxxxx
>
> X Billy's
>
> My love to all at home darling.

What thoughts must have been going through his mind as he tried (probably unsuccessfully) to snatch a couple of hours' sleep before 'going over the top'? Jack always ended his letters in similar vein (always with an extra big kiss for Billy) but he wasn't in the habit of invoking God.

31 July 1917. Passchendaele

The description which follows is taken from John Hartley's *The 6th Battalion Cheshire Regiment in the Great War.*

The assault began at 3.50 am. Two brigades advanced across No Man's Land, broke through the German front line, securing the village of St Julien just behind it. They took over 200 of the enemy prisoner. On the left, 117 Brigade also pushed forward and, with use of trench mortars and rifle grenades, rushed three concrete pillboxes and other strong-points. It had not been easy.

Once the leading troops had started their advance, a hot meal was served to all ranks in 118 Brigade. They ate it under an increasing German artillery response, which was already causing casualties. With the German front line now expected to be in British hands, the Brigade started its advance at about 5.30 am with the Cheshires on the right, with the Hertfordshire Regiment to their left. The shelling of the area by German artillery was ferocious and casualties started to mount. As planned, the three leading battalions stopped at about 6.30 am, when they reached the British front line and waited for news that the German front line had been taken.

This news came after about an hour and the advance continued. The Cheshires' line of approach brought them to the Steenbeek by 10 am – a stream, about 10 feet wide, just in front of St Julien. They crossed it on their hands and knees along a tree that had been felled.

The men reorganised and after a brief rest of after about thirty minutes, the advance resumed. Their objective was a position marked on their maps as the green line, 1100 yards north-east of St Julien. Enemy fire had been relatively light until they reached St Julien but then became very heavy.

What happened to Jack is described in a letter written to his mother in February 1919 by Corporal F Burch of the Hertfordshire Regiment.

Dear Mrs Lee,

I hope you will not think badly of me for not answering your lovely letters before, but really my time seems so full that I have had to neglect my correspondence.

Now to the best of my ability I will tell you about that fateful July 31st. Some of the things that happened I have forgotten, but the majority are of course impressed on my memory. You know of course that the 6th Cheshires and 1st Herts were brigaded together, so that by reading what my regiment did you will know what Captain Lee's did.

Our Brigade had to go over last of all in the Division, so that we had to pass through the first two Brigades on our way. Our objective was called the Langemark Line. At about 4.15 am we received our order to go over the top, and away we went. The sight which met our eyes I shall never forget, but it was also one which I cannot describe. All went well with us until we reached the half-way line, where we had to rest two hours just behind a ridge, after which we had a rather warm time, but with only two casualties. We had to take Kitchener's Wood which the Germans were shelling heavily but we got through all right. A little further on we came to the River Steenbeek which we crossed with only two more casualties although we were swept with heavy machine gun fire from the right flank. From that point we had to advance in open order, the Black Watch on the left, Herts in the centre, Cheshires on the right, and as I was in charge of the extreme right section in our regiment, I was in touch with the Cheshires all the way afterwards. Our next job was to capture the village of St Julien, the Herts and the Cheshires taking a half each, and it is needless to say that we got it. But now our real task was in front of us, the taking of the Langemark Line, and we saw that it was a stiff task, for we had to advance over 500 yards of completely flat open country, and the trench was in the form of a semi-circle, simply packed with Germans. We were immediately subjected to severe machine gun and rifle fire, and to make matters worse our own barrage was falling all amongst us and not touching the Germans. But even then all might have been well if one single British aeroplane had been above us to see what was happening. We all looked in vain though and kept on pegging away.

Hundreds had fallen or were falling, but we managed to get within 50 yards with every officer shot and almost every NCO. It was just before that that I saw your son lying in a shell hole, a shallow one, but strict orders had been issued that we were not to stay and assist wounded men as it would hinder our advance, so I had to go on. When we found we hadn't enough men to continue, we thought that the best thing to do was to get into shell holes and wait for the supports to come up, but on looking behind us to see where they were we could see only Germans – they had got in behind us and cut us off. Just at that point the order 'every man for himself' was passed down the line so we started trying to get back, at first in a group but men were falling so fast that it soon became ones and twos. At one place there were three of us in a small shell hole and we decided to try for one farther back. The other two were killed and I reached the hole alone, almost falling on top of your son who said 'hello corporal' straight away.

I set to work to see what was wrong with him and found he had been hit in the small of the back in the region of the right kidney. The wound had stopped bleeding but I could see he was badly hit internally and by the shape of the wound it was shrapnel. He told me he felt no pain whatsoever but on looking into his face I saw he was too far gone to feel anything so I cut his equipment off and removed a khaki covered steel plate which the shrapnel had penetrated, and then made a pillow for his head out of his respirator so that he could lie as comfortable as possible. Then I saw that he had begun to write a letter to his mother – it was on the back of a torn photograph of German trenches taken by one of our aeroplane observers. He finished the letter but the latter half was unintelligible and I only glanced at it as I put it in my pocket. I cannot remember any actual sentences but I know it was to the effect that he was thinking of you at the time, that he had done his bit and you were to have the MC he had won at Ypres a month before. About his wife and child I saw nothing. I did not know he was married until I received your letter in Germany, but he may well have put a message for them in the part I could not read through. If I had had the time I might have been able to decipher it. He told me to take the little gold ring off his little finger (I

remember it was so tiny it would not go on me, so I put
it in my purse and if I remember rightly it had the date
1915 on the inside). Next he asked me for a drink and
when he had had that he told me to take his revolver,
field glasses and an electric torch, and also a couple of
correspondence books which were in his pack, and send
them all with the ring and his letter to you.

He then asked me if we had taken the final objective
as it seemed to be so much quieter, which it was – I
told him we were waiting for reinforcements to come
up first. More than once he asked me for a drink, and
repeatedly said he felt no pain. I don't think he did but
he was so brave I could have cried over him. While I was
with him the Germans singled us out, and one big shell
burst within a foot of my head, but by a miracle we both
escaped. Bullets flew all round us but we were unhurt by
them, and my belief to his day is that your son was hit
by one of our own shells. So many were – the Germans
couldn't hit us.

After I had been about a quarter of an hour with
him I looked down to see that he had gone – and so
peacefully that I had not noticed it. After that I tried
the almost impossible task of getting back and, getting
into one hole after another, I at last found a comrade
in the shape of a lance corporal of the Cheshires. We
stayed together shooting Germans all around us until
four of them got quite close without our noticing them.
We immediately jumped out after them to make a fight
for it and actually reached them before we saw there
were scores of Germans lying in shell holes all around
us. The Cheshire with me took the rifle out of my hands
almost before I knew it and I remember I laughed and he
and I shook hands. The Germans (they were Saxons)

were jolly decent and only took your son's revolver from me, but everything else I had to leave behind except the ring and letter in my pocket. I saw a few more men captured round about but you will be pleased to know that none of us put our hands up.

We were escorted through 'no man's land' and along a trench to some headquarters. Here an officer who spoke excellent English was joking with us so, being afraid everything would be taken off me, I asked his advice with regard to the letter and the ring. He was full of sympathy and said he would see that you got them within three weeks if I left them with him. I could see that he was speaking the truth so I gave them to him, writing a letter to you myself to go with them. Your address I memorised and I was not likely to forget it. We had to be moved quickly after that, as our gunners began knocking the whole place to pieces with high explosives and my belief is that he must have been killed because I know he meant to keep his word, that is probably the reason why the ring and letter did not reach you.

These are all the facts I can at present think of Mrs Lee of what happened on 31 July 1917, and I tender you my deepest sympathy on losing such a brave tender son and to Mrs Jack Lee on losing a husband who was loved so much by his men. All that I have written is true, not just to show you what I did, but to tell you everything that happened as it happened, for what your son's men went through as well as myself. A man of the 6th Cheshire whose name I have forgotten but who lives near you was captured on the same day as myself, and he told me all about Captain Lee, saying how he was well loved by his men and considered the best officer in the battalion.

Any questions you like to ask I shall be only too pleased to answer to the best of my ability, and please do not think you are causing me any trouble. I am sorry I cannot give you a definite date just now for my visit to Wilmslow as I am awaiting orders for my discharge but be assured I shall manage to see you during February. With sincere regards from Miss Rendell and myself, I remain,

Yours sincerely,

F.G.Burch   1st Herts Regiment

PS I may mention that only one sergeant, two corporals and 56 men came back out of my regiment and only one corporal and myself with the men were captured. Everyone else (including officers) was killed.

And so, just like his brother-in-law two years earlier, Jack was killed within days of winning the Military Cross for bravery.

Lieutenant Frank Naden – a veteran of the Ashanti and Boer Wars – became acting commander of the 6th Battalion as the only surviving officer of the attack. On 19 August 1917 he wrote in response to a letter from Nancy:

Dear Mrs Lee,

Many thanks for your letter received today. I'm afraid up to now I can add nothing to what the colonel told you. Jack's body lies between the enemy lines and ours and will until we advance again. On doing so, I shall certainly go and see where he is buried and send you word, also get you a photograph and erect a cross. I know how much you have lost and we all feel as you do. It is only on such occasions when one has lost their all that one realises what war is and no monetary considerations can recompense one for the love that one has lost.

Speaking officially, and it is necessarily so, you are entitled to a pension for yourself and child and gratuity of a captain. Any other information I shall get I should only be too pleased to send you. His personal effects were sent to Cox's on the 14th of this month and you should receive them ere long.

In conclusion I can only express my deepest sympathy with you in this your terrible loss.

Sincerely yours

F Naden

We lost 17 officers and 495 men. Only myself and R Morton and about 100 men came back.

Jack's body was never recovered and he is one of the 55,000 soldiers commemorated on the Menin Gate.

My father – 'Billy' – had been registered as William Barrie Lee, but 'Jack' was subsequently added by hand to his birth certificate and he became William Jack Barrie Lee. From that time, he was known to his family as Jack.

6

RALPH

During the summer holiday at the end of his first year at Glasgow University, Ralph Erskine was on a walking holiday on the Isle of Arran with his good friend Charles Higgins when war broke out. They both immediately headed home to join up. Ralph joined the 7th Battalion of the Royal Scots Fusiliers which was formed in Ayr, and was posted to Aldershot for training.

Ralph wrote to his father in October 1914, saying:

> Things are going all right here, only our officers are very incompetent, the company major and captain know next to nothing about the work and of course it doesn't have the effect of inspiring confidence in us and in the men.

A few days later he witnessed a gruesome accident, described in a letter to Tommy.

> Last night a terrible thing happened. When we were at tea, word came in that an aeroplane had caught fire and was sinking. I rushed out and in that time it had

dropped like a wounded bird some two miles away. There was a general exodus from camp and, of course, I was among the first to get there, by which time hundreds of troops from neighbouring camps had gathered at a distance of about 200 yards from the flaming pile. Only officers and doctors were allowed near and when I got near I saw a human head, charred and black and hairless, sticking out of the flames. Oh Tommy, it was the most awful sight I have ever seen. Before we could extricate him we had to break the burning mass from above him. Both his legs were smashed to bits. Seemingly, from those who had seen him in the air, he had controlled the machine for about two miles after it had caught fire and then, overcome, he and the machine plunged to earth. Of course he was dead long before he reached earth. His name was Busk and he had been at it for 4 years. He was an expert tester.

The unfortunate victim had the unusual name of Edward Teshmaker Busk and he had been a distinguished designer and test pilot at the Royal Aircraft Factory in Farnborough.

A letter to his father showed Ralph already had higher ambitions.

We have been told that names had been taken for those who wished to volunteer as aircraft observers. Three men gave their names. If there is another chance I should very much like to put my name in. What do you think? It would mean that we'd get to France much sooner than otherwise. Thanks very much for the nice boots. They are just the thing. We move to huts on Saturday. Bramshott is the name of the place.

A few days later to his father:

> We go into huts on Monday and it will be much better. It has been bitterly cold here these last two days but very healthy indeed.
>
> When I get to Bramshott I would like you to send me a bottle of brown polish, medium colour. I like to keep up appearances here and everybody envies me my shoes.
>
> I think my uniform is about the best out of the whole lot and yet some of them have paid more than double. I think I shall get my next winter tunic in Mosses. They have great stocks ready-made.
>
> This morning we had a splendid route march but of course our intelligent captain and major led us all wrong.

In November 1914 Ralph moved to Bramshott, near Liphook.

> We shifted here yesterday and it is indeed a pleasant change, although still rough. At this point we are about 16 miles from Aldershot and 26 from Portsmouth and we are about 800 feet high. The country around is beautiful, moorland and copses interspersed and all over the place are very nice hotels and country houses. It has been bitterly cold since we arrived. The Huts are not nearly finished off yet. By that I mean that there are no stones. It is ever so much colder than in tents. Of course the climate is quite different. We all wakened with the cold last night. There have never been any camps here before, so I judge from the look of the ground, and now there is a very compact colony of huts each of which holds 40 men. In all there are 1600 men, that is two divisions I think. My men were nearly

all frozen last night, they get three blankets each. But tonight they have paillasses raised off the floor so I hope it will be better. We shall get very hard here and healthy.

Then Ralph showed his soft side.

I am very happy here but at times I feel lonely and long to see your dear old face. Last night in the hotel when we were having music I thought of you and I went away and had a wee cry.

A few days later:

I have just come in after a very stiff route march and am quite ready for lunch.

The country here is quite different to anywhere I have ever seen, but it is very fine. A keen frost has prevailed till this morning, when it threatens snow.

I have just heated a brick and am sitting with my feet resting on it and it is very cosy indeed.

30 November 1914

My dear Daddy,

I just got your letter this morning and was very glad to get it, but I am sorry to hear that you haven't yet got any work to do. It has been very wet here for the last week and now the ground between the huts is in a most terrific mess. Without exaggeration it is ankle deep. We had to spend the whole forenoon in the hut for lectures and now we have a half holiday to celebrate St Andrews Day. Tonight is my first guest night and everything is being got shipshape. Of course we have haggis tonight. Everything you sent I have received, polish, watch etc.

O! I have learned to ride. It's splendid. Some of the men have been up repeatedly and haven't reached a gallop yet. I was galloping within 5 mins of mounting. I just made up my mind to say nothing and go about it as if I was quite used to it. I mounted at the stables and had to take the horse right round the camp to a field behind. I wanted something soft to fall on. The nearest I had to falling was caused by the horse galloping into a tree and my eye was cut by a branch. And yet I wasn't a bit frightened. I have made up my mind to funk at nothing.

I get on very well with the colonel now. He was telling me last night that one of his previous sub-lieutenants, Utterson Kelso, was shot through the neck and tonsils and he tumbled forwards into a trench. He lay there for hours with two or three dead gunners over him. Then in the evening he came to and went back among the men.

As time went on, conditions improved.

Things are being licked into shape here now. We have now a large stove in our hut, and hence the place is much cosier. This morning I accompanied our captain on a reconnoitring walk. We were scouring new country and looking for good places to train, and this is admirable country for that. We walked about 12 miles before lunch. The country is wild and nearly all bracken and heather and then dense woods. When entering a glen I suddenly heard a sharp chopping sound. I immediately guessed it to be caused by a woodpecker. We stole quietly up but it flew away as we neared.

This afternoon we had a terrific route march to the highest point in the whole county. Its height is 895 feet and southwards stretches across the South Downs to Portsmouth on the right and to Brighton on the left. And on the other side it rolls away towards Oxford. Just west there is a huge valley called the Devil's Punchbowl and it looked truly wild today in the grey light.

In February 1915 Ralph's battalion was moved to Basingstoke, then to Draycott Camp near Swindon. In the same month he was promoted to lieutenant.

He wrote to Nancy.

I am resting this afternoon to be fresh tonight for night work. We shall be out all night. Tomorrow, Saturday, I am going to Wimbledon. Lennie, another girl and Charlie (Higgins) are going to the Savoy Dance at night. This I think will be my last time before we go. We shall go in about 4 or 5 weeks. I hear quite often from Tommy. I'm glad he has had a change of work.

I got a letter from Betty some time ago in which she said Daddy was leaving for the Sportsmans Battalion last Monday. Since then I have not heard from him but I presume he is somewhere around London. I shall try tomorrow when I am up to find his whereabouts. Now, Nancy, before going out we are given at least 48 hours leave, and if Daddy has gone I will have no place to go unless to some friends in London. Now I might try to get to Aberystwyth for a day. I suppose there is some hotel there. Or against that you might come to London for a day or two, we might live at Higgins or at some hotel. What do you say? That of course is if 8 Deerpark is shut. For home is home.

We are in huts here but the huts are much better than those we vacated at Bramshott.

Lennie was Jane Lennox Higgins, the sister of his friend Charles Higgins, with whom he had been walking on Arran when war broke out.

A few weeks later Ralph was posted to France. The next letters we have are after Tommy was killed.

20 August 1915

Dear Wee Sister,

I'm back in billets again after having been in the front line for 8 days. They were fairly uneventful days although we had a few casualties. One sergeant killed, 1 officer and 4 men wounded and then our company commander was shot through the foot. Previously to going up to the trenches our colonel was killed by a shell and our doctor severely wounded. Since then he has had his leg amputated. The shell burst about 50 yards away from me but fortunately I was in a dug-out. So should they have been. It is nice to be back again and I'm enjoying the rest.

I haven't heard from Charlie Higgins for 10 days and previously he'd been writing constantly. The Dardanelles seem to be a death trap. Poor wee Chas, I hope he gets through all right*.

Daddy seems to be having a great deal of worry and annoyance about his commission. The fact of his not

---

*Charlie wasn't alright. Serving at Gallipoli, he had been wounded a few days earlier at Suvla Bay. He was repatriated and made a full recovery.

having got his uniform must be a source of great worry. I do hope he gets it as it will be the only thing to keep his mind occupied.

How are you enjoying Auchterarder? How do you spend your time?

Write soon Nancy dear to your loving brother
Ralph

23 August 1915

Your letter arrived this morning and I was glad to get it. You must be down-hearted at your present state. It is only temporary and the work in the fields will do you a world of good. The fact that you are dog tired at night is a good sign.

This will only be a short note just now as I am taking out a working party tonight to dig communication trenches. At present we are back in billets resting after eight days in the trenches.

18 September 1915

Just a wee note as time will not allow for more and in any case there is little to tell. We are having a quiet life just now, the calm before the storm. I like storms. We are going to move them this time.

Charlie Higgins is doing well in the 3 General London Hospital, Wandsworth. You should write to him. He would be awfully bucked.

No more just now dearie, I am going to do some bombing this afternoon so au revoir.

Ralph was soon involved in more action.

1 October 1915

> Dearie,
> Just a wee note. I know I wrote you a letter the other day but what I said in it I haven't got the slightest idea. My brain was all in a whirl and even yet back resting I can't get the noise of battle out of my ears. I wrote to Betty and also to Daddy. He is now at Scone. Write to me soon dearie. I shall never, if I can help it, go back to Glasgow again. I am sick of it and its association. In any case there are many more fights to be fought.

Ralph had been taking part in the Battle of Loos, the biggest British attack of 1915, an attempt to break through the German defences in Artois and Champagne. It was unsuccessful, and British casualties were twice as high as German losses.

5 October 1915

> Dear wee Nancy,
> Just a wee note. Leave has started today. Arthur has gone, he returns on the 12th. When do you go to Aber and when can you come to London for a day or two? I don't want to go to Glasgow. Let me know at once please.
> Fondest love
> Ralph.

Meanwhile Ralph's relationship with Lennie had become serious.

16 December 1915

Darling sister,

Thank you again and again for your letter. It did me a great deal of good and cheered me just when I wanted it.

It isn't going to be easy nevertheless. Mr Higgins approves of me alright but of course it is the want of the goods and all very natural. He seems very determined and I shall challenge him when I go home again. But I don't care if she had a thousand fathers all saying no, I'd marry her.

You know dear, Tommy's death is the first thing that has made me realise that I am grown up. Yes Nancy we will try to make our dear old Daddy ever so happy. You mustn't mention this matter to a soul.

We are now back in billets. We came in yesterday and shall be here for a month so that's all right.

Now write to me often.

The helmet is splendid.

A few days later Ralph was posted to the Royal Flying Corps as an observer.

Dearest Daddy,

Just a wee note. I had an order today to report myself at HQ RFC on Monday 27th to commence duties as observer so that will commence a new chapter of my life. I think I shall enjoy it all right even though I never did like heights.

We are enjoying the rest immensely and are taking things fairly easily although when we work we work hard. I am hoping to hear from you soon. I really don't know anything about pay etc in the new job.

Write soon again Daddy dear.

Your boy Ralph

Before joining the RFC, Ralph showed his vulnerable side.

Dear Old Daddy,

There are times I feel so lonely and I just long to have you to cuddle. One night I have dreaming, half waking, thought how glorious it would be if we could be together. Life would never be dull or grey if we could fight together and we'd fear nothing on this earth. I thought about it so much I almost imagined it true. But now that dream is ended as I go to the RFC unless you could come there. There have been older men have started and what anyone of 40 can do, you can do. Still if you are happy, that is the main thing.

I am writing this in bed and beginning to feel tired. If only you were here you could cuddle me.

Goodnight my Daddy,

Your loving boy

Ralph

Within weeks of starting as an observer, Ralph had an unfortunate encounter with a famous German fighter ace. A contemporary source described what happened.

On 14 January 1916 Lieutenant Justin Howard Herring took off in BE2c No. 4087 with his observer, Captain Ralph Erskine. They were both lucky to survive the day, as they encountered the man largely credited with the invention of fighter tactics, Oswald Boelcke.

An hour into their reconnaissance mission Boelcke came across Herring's BE2c near Achiet-le-Grand (just north of Bapaume in the Pas de Calais). After what Boelcke stated was his most difficult combat up to that time, the BE2c crashed just in front of the barbed-wire protecting the British front-line trenches, leaving Herring and Erskine scrambling for the safety of the British lines.

They came down in part of the line held by the 7th Battalion, East Kent Regiment, as recorded in their war diary.

'Our aircraft No 4087 of 8 Squadron came down in our lines after being hit near Bapaume and attacked by 4 Fokker machines. Pilot Lt Herring and Observer Captain Erskine both wounded but got out of the machine and into the trenches. Machine shelled by Germans. First hit registered after 35 shells. We did for good execution *(sic)* with shrapnel on their front line as their infantry manned the trenches and looked over the parapet. During the day they fired over 250 shells at the machine. We suffered some casualties 1 killed and 2 wounded: 2 nights after we managed to salve 2 Machine guns and the compass. Various odd pieces now adorn the walls of Becourt Chateau as mementoes.'

Boelcke allegedly ended the day in the rather more comfortable surroundings of a dinner with the King of Bavaria! He subsequently claimed 40 'kills' before himself being killed in a mid-air collision on 28 October 1916. Major Justin Howard Herring was fortunate to survive his encounter with Oswald Boelcke and went on to win a DSO in Mesopotamia to add to the MC he'd already won in France. He ended the war as the commanding officer of the RAF air station at Hucknall.

The War Office sent a telegram to Granddaddy saying Ralph had been admitted to Rouen General Hospital with a gunshot wound in his right leg.

Ralph made a good recovery. His next letter is four months later.

Sunday 28 May

No 8 Squadron RFC

Dearest Nancy,

I have been expecting to hear from you for some time now but no letter arrives.

I am enjoying life very much out here and the flying these days is glorious.

I have not yet had the news of cousin Tommy's* death confirmed. It is too terrible to believe. Still it is better not to think of these things.

How is Jack? Write and give me all the news. Have you written to Minnie Erskine recently? I wish you would.

I am getting a fair amount of flying to do, about two hours a day. There are so many observers out now.

Write soon to your own brother
Ralph

Meanwhile Lennie confided in a letter to Nancy how much she was missing Ralph.

Dearest Nancy,

I've been wondering how you are and what you're doing – I know I can't expect a letter from you because I never answered your last one. I have been very lonely since Ralph went back to France, I miss him more than anyone knows. I saw a good deal of him before he went

---

* *Tommy Barrie was Ralph's cousin who had been killed in France on 5 May 1916 aged 24. He is buried at Vermelles Cemetery in the Pas-de-Calais.*

and we were so happy. Of course I write to him every day and try not to worry – but he's so far away. If only I knew he were safe it wouldn't matter so much.

Later Ralph wrote to Nancy while she was working on a farm.

30 July 1916

I was so glad to see from your letter that you are thriving on the work. It is the best thing you could do and it makes me happy to know that you are happy. I can see reason in it all. Doesn't Jack want to farm after the war? How is he? What regiment is he in? Is he near the battle at present?

Lennie has been at Lamlash* for a month and is now going home. She will likely have written you by this time.

This is a glorious day, an ideal Sunday.

Ralph finally overcame any parental objections and in December he and Lennie became engaged. They were married on 9 March 1917 at St Columba's Church in Pont Street, one of only two Church of Scotland churches in London.

Ralph returned to his flying duties and graduated from observer to pilot. He was based at Dartford, one of the RFC's early bases, when he heard of Jack's death.

63 Training Squadron R.F.C., Joyce Green, Dartford Aug 8th

Nancy Darling,

I got the news from Lennie today by phone. I have just wired you. I shall come up as soon as possible. I

---

* *The battle referred to was the Somme. Lamlash is the largest village on the Isle of Arran.*

can't get away tonight because there must be a certain number of trained pilots for home defence. But I may get away tomorrow. I can't say anything. I just want to be with you and I will soon.

Your loving brother

Ralph

Ralph visited Nancy at Wilmslow then wrote again.

15 August 1917

Dearest Wee Sister,

I am just snatching a moment in which to write you. Flying has ceased for the moment because of the showers.

I should love to be with you again cuddling that dear wee boy.

I was glad to find you all so brave. You must always keep busy and never allow yourself to dwell too long on things. That seems on the surface wrong and selfish but it isn't. Mrs Lee is a dear brave old woman and I have great admiration for her. It is a great comfort to know that you are among such sterling people, and always remember darling that you have me whenever you want. It is going to be one of my duties and greatest pleasures to be with you and help you whenever I can. We must stick very closely to each other. Give the little one a hug from me.

And give my love to all.

Your own brother

Ralph

I left my strop behind the bathroom door. Please send it.

15 September 1917

Once again my appalling memory played me false and so the stocking would be a bit late in arriving. I'd have written sooner but yesterday I was on home defence at Croydon aerodrome, I came back here again this morning.

I hope you are well darling and getting out into the fresh air as much as possible. You must still take lots of exercise and keep strong.

On 22 September 1917, having completed his training, Ralph was posted to 66 Squadron, which had been formed the previous year in Filton, Bristol. The squadron was now operating in Estree-Blanche in northern France.

A week later Ralph was flying a patrol over the Menin Road in Flanders with a naturalised Italian called Tone Bayetto, who before the war had been a racing driver and a head waiter at the Carlton Hotel in Haymarket. This account is taken from the Facebook page of an organisation called Historians Inc.

On 30 September Tone in B2168 whilst on patrol with 2/ Lt Joseph G. Warter in B2185 and James W. Boumphrey in B1768, Howard K Boysen in B2176, Ralph Erskine in B2189, Lancelot May in B2221 and Walabanke A Pritt in B2162. The patrol was engaged by 15 enemy aircraft from above near the Menin-Roulers Road, one of the e.a. (enemy aircraft) positioned behind Bayetto, but he was able to evade the attack, he then closed on another e.a who was on the tail of one of the patrol Pups, Bayetto was unable to fire on this e.a. and it shot down the Pup in flames. He saw another Pup with two e.a. on its tail, diving towards the group, he closed to within

30 feet and fired on the enemy, he watched the tracer entering the fuselage just behind the pilot, the pilot looked behind and saw Bayetto, the pilot then slumped over the side of the cockpit, the e.a. machine started to descend and signs of smoke were observed. Tone levelled out at 8000 feet, hearing machine guns he looked around to find another e.a. diving on him, Tone performed an Immelmann*, getting behind the e.a. he fired a short burst into the machine, the propeller was seen to stop and the e.a. started to make for the east, at the same time a two seater opened fire on Tone from underneath the Pup shooting away one of his cylinders and tearing away his cowling, piercing his petrol tank and shooting two blades off his propeller, he was then attacked by another Albatross, who shot him up his left rear spar, which resulted in the spar and several wing ribs breaking. In one of his accounts of the action, he says that the patrol was attacked by 26 enemy machines. He was shot about and flew the aeroplane upside down and attempted to right the craft shortly before landing the aircraft, which in another account is said to have pancaked the machine from 20 feet in amongst shell holes, as he crashed Tone's face hit the windscreen and Lewis gun butt, the fuselage compressed the cockpit and the undercarriage collapsed the machine overturned on its nose. He was unconscious for about 20 minutes before being rescued, he sustained impact wounds to his face and back, he was unconscious for a while and bled from his left ear, nose and mouth, he was later found to be suffering from a fractured skull and suffered severe bruising, not surprisingly he also suffered from headaches, hearing and eyesight

---

*An Immelmann turn is an aeronautical manoeuvre, named after a German fighter ace, which results in flying in the opposite direction at a higher altitude.

problems for a while. He was sent back down the lines and was admitted to 7 General Hospital in St Omer before he returned to Home Establishment via Calais and Dover on 18 October.

By now Ralph had another factor in his life – Lennie was expecting their first child.

12 October 1917

My darling wee sister,

I have delayed writing till I knew you were at Glenafton *(Lennie's family home in Wimbledon)*. I am so glad you are there. The change will do you good and you will be such a help for Lennie.

Yes darling, I know you love me and I love you and would do anything in the world for you. I only want, some day, to be able to show you how much I care for you.

When I was home I was looking forward more than I can say to your visit and I only wish I were there now. We'd have been so happy all together. I want so much to see that wee darling of yours. You know it won't be so very long till I get leave. If only you could stay a month or so. I have twice tried to find Tommy's grave but duty in the first case and darkness in the second prevented me.

I think you will find Lennie much happier than she was and in any case you are a brave wee girl and will help her. She has been looking forward day by day to your arrival so now she will be happy.

But this must go to the mail so goodnight brave little sister.

Your brother

Ralph

14 October 1917

Darling Sister,

Lennie says you are thinner than you were when I saw you. Try not to worry darling. Are you still feeding baby? You will fatten afterwards.

How I wish I were with you. How strange Glenafton will be with a baby's voice in it calling and crying. But of course your baby doesn't cry.

You mustn't let him forget me darling. Keep telling him about me.

I'm going to make you happy after this business little philosopher.

Write and tell me about Lennie.

Your fond brother

Ralph.

19 October 1917

Nancy darling,

When I read your letters except for the writing I might be reading my Daddy's. You say things the same way my darling.

But I'm worried about you my dearie, you must put on weight. I hope you have got rid of that cold and the headaches.

Yes my wee Lennie is alright, isn't she? Just as straight as a die. I'm glad she is so well as she is exceptionally strong.

Hug the wee one for me.

Your loving brother

Ralph

November brought the Russian revolution. With a lessening of pressure on the eastern front the Germans took the opportunity to assist their Austro-Hungarian allies on the Italian front, where a fierce war was being waged at high altitude in the Alps. As a consequence, the allies diverted some resources from the western front to Italy.

On 22 November Ralph's 66 Squadron was transferred to Milan, and then a week later to Verona, where they were based on the racecourse. On 4 December they moved to Grossa, just east of Vicenza, and from then onwards were involved in the main military action which was taking place a few miles away on the River Piave.

On 16 December the 66 Squadron website records that Ralph claimed a 'kill'.

It simply notes: At 13:05:00. Erskine, R in B3931 *(a Sopwith Camel)*.

Ralph's next letter was written over two days.

Sunday 16 December

Dear wee sister,

I have the photo of you and your wee boy here before me and I kiss it again and again. It is sweet of you both and framed. I'm so glad to see you are much stronger.

I was so glad to get your letter. I wish you'd write me oftener. It is cold here now and having no comforts writing is a trying business. The objective here was to own the Rhone Valley and along the Riviera.

But it is late now and I am out early in the morning. I will write more tomorrow when I have more time.

Goodnight darling

(Next day)

Dearie – there is little to tell.

The Hun doesn't show himself much these days. We frightened him pretty soon.

I'll be glad when summer comes. It is evening now and I have been at it all day and must now go round to the mess to see if there is any food to be had.

I got a long letter from Daddy yesterday. I hope you send him a copy of the photos.

Lennie seems to be wonderfully well still. Yes she is very unlike her parents and yet after a bit you see parts of resemblance especially to Mr Higgins.

Give my love to Aunty and Uncle and heaps to yourself.

Your loving brother

Ralph

We next hear of Ralph in a short biography of a Scottish pilot called Wilfred George Robinson Bailes, known as 'Robin' who, before joining the RFC, had fought at Messines and contracted trench foot.

On 26 December Lt. Ralph Erskine commanded the second patrol of the day. The other members were 2/Lt's. A. F. Bartlett, A.B. Reade and Robin in Camel B5407. They departed at 10.00 am but Robin crashed on take-off and according to the squadron record book he sustained severe facial injuries and a broken leg. Robin's war was over after 10 sorties and 26 hours flying time.

The following day Ralph wrote to Nancy before a two-mile walk for his supper.

66 Squadron RFC
BEF Italy
27/12/17

Darling little sister,

Just a wee note to say that I'm still very fit and well and hoping to have leave very shortly, even in time to be home with Lennie. I have little time for long letter writing here and when I do have it the conditions are so uncongenial. I mean it's so cold and fires are very few and far between in this frugal land. Fortunately winter only lasts two months more and then comes their beautiful spring. These days the Alps are whiter than ever and morning and evening we enjoy pictures of nature indescribably beautiful.

The old Hun avoids us and won't often do battle because the few times that he has he has gone under and down.

Lennie sent me a beautiful snap of baby taken at Embersons. It's just great and I love it.

I hope you are well darling and not neglecting in any way to exercise and get fresh air. You certainly made a great hit at Glenafton with that dear wee boy of yours.

But now dearie my feet are getting cold and my tummy is becoming gradually emptier so I must now walk the two miles between me and supper,

Goodnight my wi' Nancy, with my love to Auntie and Uncle,

Your loving brother
Ralph

Please give me news of the Barries, all of them, Uncle Alex, Johnny, Bobby, Hendry, Cousin Jeannie, Peggy, the American, them all.

Tragically, that was his last letter to her.

On New Year's Day 1918, Ralph climbed into the cockpit of Sopwith Camel B6414, and took off from Grossa in support of 42 Squadron on a bombing mission. His group of three Camels was attacked by 15 Albatross D.III Scouts, and his aircraft was last seen at 6000 feet over Vittorio in pursuit of one of them. His brother-in-law and best friend Charles Higgins subsequently wrote that he was not carrying a parachute, and this appears to have been generally the case at that time.

Despite its brutality, there was still room for chivalry in this war. The day after Ralph's aircraft went missing, the Austro-Hungarians dropped a package behind allied lines containing his personal effects and this message:

> Captain Ralph Erskine, died from wounds, buried with military honours San Fior 2/1/18.

A full week after the information from the enemy about Ralph's burial, the War Office got round to notifying his father by telegram.

> Regret to inform that Capt R Erskine General List RFC 66 Squad is reported missing January first. This does not necessarily mean either killed or wounded. Further news will be sent immediately received.

The telegram still only says he's missing, though by this time his family must have been fearing the worst.

The following day they got round to sending the same message to Lennie.

Still without official confirmation of Ralph's death, on 16 January, fifteen days after he was shot down, Lennie had her baby at their home in Church Road, Wimbledon. It was a boy named Ralph Barrie Erskine, always known as Barrie. When she registered the birth eight days later, the father was listed as 'Captain RFC, Medical student'.

It was another month before the dreadful news was officially confirmed. Granddaddy wrote to Nancy.

My dear wee Nancy,

I have just received bad news from Lennie's father. He has been told unofficially that a message has come through Copenhagen stating that a Captain Erskine and another RFC officer (whose name is illegible) were killed and buried together.

I know you will be deeply grieved – what can we do or say.

My heart is sold for Lennie and for you (who both loved him so dearly). I hope you will be able to comfort each other from the depth of your great sorrow. For me – 'the rest is silence'.

Your always loving
Daddy

Ralph was the first RFC fatality of the Italian campaign.

A couple of months later came a final bureaucratic absurdity – the War Office wrote crediting four (old!) pence to Ralph's mess account for his lunch allowance on the day he was shot down.

Ralph's official grave is at the small but beautifully kept Commonwealth War Graves Commission Cemetery at Tezze, to the north-east of Vicenza. But there are doubts as to the actual location of his remains, as evidenced by this mysterious letter from a Romanian Major in the Austro-Hungarian Army sent to the War Office in Isleworth in 1926, which was translated by them.

I, the undersigned, Major P Balica, beg to express my thanks for the information received in the letter No 37830/7 (R.Records) of 18.3.1926 and ask that the enclosed photograph and the following memorandum may be forwarded to the late hero, Captain Ralph Erskine, and the receipt of the same acknowledged.

Memorandum

It is with a certain feeling of emotion that I forward the enclosed photograph, showing the grave of Capt. Ralph Erskine which may, perhaps for the first time, give some comforts to his parents and relatives in need of consolation.

It is my duty to state how this photograph was discovered.

There is living with us at Orovita a widow named Andrekovich Victoria, 60 years of age, who lost her only son in the Great War. As I knew her son very well, she sent me many picture postcards and photographs, amongst which I found the enclosed, and which – in accordance with the dictates of chivalry and humanity – I cannot keep in my album or my possession. I therefore place them at the disposal of the rightful owners.

Neither the old woman nor I can give any information as to the situation of the grave in question, or the theatre of war with which it is connected, but no doubt the British War Office could at once identify it.

Since the old widow Andrekovich Victoria is quite alone, and in consequence of the revolution which occurred here in 1918, is left without means in these difficult times, I ask if she may be granted a little assistance in return.

Hoping that I have fulfilled my duty, in accordance with the dictates of honour and humanity, I have the honour, etc
Major P Balica

Sadly, the photograph has not survived. Were Ralph's remains transferred to Tezze, or does he still lie near Flor, where the Austro-Hungarians originally buried him?

7

AFTER THE GREAT
WAR

The armistice of 11 November 1918 brought the Great War to an end, but not before it had claimed another member of Granddaddy's family.

His brother-in-law Alexander Barrie, serving as a corporal in the 2nd Highland Infantry, was killed in action in France only six weeks before the end of hostilities. Another sporting member of the family, Alexander – known as 'Lachie' – had played professional football for Rangers, Kilmarnock, and finally for several years in England for Sunderland, where he earned the dubious distinction of being only the second player from that club to be sent off! I had the honour of laying a wreath at the club war memorial at the Stadium of Light in 2018, where I was generously hosted at the subsequent match by the club's legendary goalkeeper Jim Montgomery.

The extensive involvement of the Barrie family in the war is listed in Appendix B.

Granddaddy was demobbed. He had started the war with two sons and a daughter. At the end he just had Nancy, a widowed single mother who had just turned 21. One can only begin to imagine his state of mind.

He had already started a long correspondence with the War Office about Tommy. He had three issues. The first was a desire for proper recognition of Tommy's supreme bravery in the shape of a Victoria Cross or at least a Distinguished Service Order to add to his Military Cross. I'm no expert in bravery awards but from the description of his actions, a VC does not sound out of order. The second was about Tommy's rank. He had been promoted to Captain the day before he was killed but the formalities hadn't gone through. And finally his status – was he a reservist or a regular? This affected his gratuity. The War Office took a bureaucratic line and Granddaddy, a good 'barrack room lawyer', argued his case tenaciously.

To: The Secretary,
War Office,
27 June 1917

Sir, Reference M.S.3.a

I have the honour to acknowledge receipt of your memo of 16/6/17, requesting a reply to your letter of 30/5/17. As the latter, however, does not appear to call for any reply, I presume the reference is to your previous letter of 29/3/17, which was answered in the first paragraph of mine of 25/5/17.

If my preference for receiving my son's decoration at the hands of His Majesty the King cannot be complied with, my next choice would be to have it presented in Glasgow, my son's native city.

With reference to your letter of 2/6/17 on the subject of the Victoria Cross, I am not in touch with the Officer who was in command of the 1st Gordon

Highlanders at the time of my son's death, and who recommended him for the Distinguished Service Order. I would therefore respectfully suggest that this officer – Lt Colonel P W Brown – should be informed by you of the fact that his recommendation for a posthumous award was abortive, and requested to submit any recommendation he might wish to make regarding the Victoria Cross through the usual and necessary channels. General A E Hoskins was in command of the 8th Brigade, and knew all the circumstances. He would, I have no doubt, confirm any such recommendation.

> I have the honour to be,
> Sir,
> Your obedient servant,
> J Erskine, Captain
> Station Bombing Officer
> Highland Territorial Force Reserve Brigade
> Ripon

The Army's position was expressed thus in an internal memo:

This officer was selected for a permanent commission on 19 July 1915

Submitted to King on 26 July 1915

Gazetted 27 July 1915

In accordance with precedent, Gazette notice will be cancelled as this officer never did duty in his new appointment.

Section 34A refers.

If you agree please action as to cancellation of Gazette.

Two months later Granddaddy returned serve.

1 September 1917

Sir,

I have the honour to acknowledge receipt of your letter of 29/8/17 which, however, I regret is not understood.

My son, Thomas Barrie Erskine, was appointed on 14 August 1914 as a 2/Lt in the Special Reserve of Officers. He was afterwards promoted to the rank of Lt and later to that of Captain. I hold from you a letter (the date of which I am unable to quote as it is not in my possession) informing me definitely, in reply to a query, that at the time of his death he held the rank of Captain. Your designation of him as 2/Lt would therefore appear to be incorrect.

I am aware that shortly before he was killed he applied for a Commission in the Regular Army and that, posthumously I think, he was gazetted 2/Lt 1st Gordon Highlanders; but that circumstance does not alter the fact that he was originally appointed, and served, as an officer of the Special Reserve of Officers, 'taken into employment by reason of a National Emergency' and 'employed with' the 'Regular Army'.

It would appear therefore that the gratuity allowed under Article 497 Pay Warrant fell to be paid to his estate, and that the payments you have already made were admissible.

I shall be pleased to hear that you concur, and to receive a draft for the balance of £13.5.9 still unpaid, and the additional sum of £5.3.6 which has accrued (as shown in your letter), a total of £18.9.3.

After the war Granddaddy took up the cudgels again, going straight to the top!

To: The Rt Honourable Winston S Churchill Esq,
Secretary of State for War,
London
15 December 1920

Dear Mr Churchill,

I have just received from the War Office a card bearing your signature intimating that my son, Lt (later Capt) T B Erskine (died of wounds) was mentioned in despatches on 30 November 1915. He is designated on this card as 'Argyll & Sutherland Highlanders'. As this designation opens up a prolonged but fruitless discussion I had with the Financial Secretary I am taking the opportunity to bring this to your notice. My son, with his brother (who was also killed in the war), was a student at Glasgow University and a member of the OTC (Officers Training Corps). He joined up on 4 August 1914 as an officer of the Reserve of Officers. He was attached thereafter to the 1st Gordon Highlanders, with which regiment he served until his death on 19 July 1915. He was awarded the Military Cross earlier in 1915 and recommended posthumously for the Distinguished Service Order. Sometime before his death he was recommended by his Commanding Officer to apply for a regular commission so that he might be permanently attached to the Gordon Highlanders.

He did so, and was posthumously gazetted to a regular commission. He however joined up, served, and died as an Officer of the Reserve, 'employed in a time of national emergency'. He had no intention of remaining in the Army as his university course was finished and he had earned his degree of MA. *(It was conferred posthumously, with first class honours.)* In the circumstances, he clearly came under the provision of Article 493 Pay Warrant for the purpose of gratuity; but the Financial Secretary, (against the spirit and the content of the Royal Warrant) insists that as his commission to the regulars (though gazetted posthumously) was dated before his death he does not come under the provisions of the Royal Warrant. What frustrates me is that for every other purpose than the payment of gratuity he is (as on the card which is the occasion of this letter) designated as being an officer of the Argyll & Sutherland Highlanders. Might I ask you to look into this matter personally? The correspondence will be found under the number 47053/3 (Accts 4).

I have mentioned that my son was recommended posthumously for the DSO. Sometime in 1916 or 1917 it was stated in the House of Commons (in answer to a question) that the matter of posthumous DSOs would be gone into at the conclusion of the war. I accordingly took no further steps at this time; but when (after receiving the MC at the hands of His Majesty the King) I communicated with the War Office on this subject, I was informed that no posthumous DSOs were to be conferred.

I pointed out that, had his C/O known that his recommendation would be abortive, he would no doubt have nominated him for the VC. There is good reason for believing that the War Office said that if the C/O recommended it, the matter would be considered. I have never taken any further steps, as I consider it would be inappropriate for me to approach his C/O on such a matter. The latter is now Lt-Col P W Brown, now in command of the 2nd Gordon Highlanders, stationed at Maryhill Barracks, Glasgow.

Since I have trespassed so far on your good nature, perhaps you will forgive me if I go a little further still, and ask your advice on another matter. At the end of 1914, both my sons having joined up, I applied for a commission and in September 1915 was gazetted to the 7th Gordon Highlanders. I served successively as Battalion, Brigade, and Divisional Bombing Officer, and later as Assistant Brigade Major.

I was never allowed (on account of my age – I am 55) to proceed overseas. Like many other Scotsmen I had devoted my income in pre-war years to the education of my family, and my two sons were my only assets in the world. (A penny for Nancy's thoughts about this. RL) Since demobilisation I have had no employment of any kind and no income, with the result that I am nearing the end of my tether. I have had no gratuity of any kind. Is there, do you think, any chance of my being granted a pension in respect of my son's death? I should add that my younger son (he was the first RFC casualty in Italy on 1 January 1918) was married, so his widow and son receive his pension.

With apologies for troubling you with this long letter.
I am,
Your obedient servant,
James Erskine,
Late Captain Gordon Highlanders.

Granddaddy certainly had the all the qualities of a good trade union shop steward – clever, articulate, stubborn. But it is doubtful if this well-argued letter ever reached Churchill's desk. An inappropriately named underling batted it back in a few lengthy sentences.

18 January 1921

Dear Sir,

Mr Churchill asks me to refer to your letter of 15 December 1920, and to say that he has made enquiries and finds that Lieutenant Erskine had applied for a regular commission a short time before his death and his application was granted from a date prior to his death, although the Gazette notice did not appear till shortly afterwards.

Mr Churchill is afraid that under these circumstances it will be impossible to issue a gratuity under Article 497 of the Pay Warrant, and only the Regular Army Officer's Gratuity under Army Order 85 of 1919 is payable.

In the case of officers promoted from the ranks who have been killed before the appearance of the Gazette notice, the War Office always honours the Gazette and treats them as officers for financial benefits. It is therefore not considered possible to take a different line in respect of applications for permanent commissions.

Mr Churchill is therefore afraid that there is no method by which you can benefit from Army funds.

Yours faithfully,

O.S. Cleverly

Private Secretary

Despite his forceful advocacy, Granddaddy got nowhere against the Whitehall bureaucracy. Frustrated by the attitude of the War Office, and disillusioned with life in general, he turned his back on life in the city.

With his small war pension and a little income from his father-in-law's estate, he built himself a wooden chalet on the top of Cathkin's Brae above Rutherglen at Rogerton, and adopted the life of a recluse. The two-roomed dwelling stood amongst the heather near a knoll of trees, and was very basic, with no proper sanitation drainage, and water being collected from the roof. Like most rural areas, it didn't get electricity until the late 1930s.

Books were stacked from floor to ceiling in the living room, where Granddaddy would sit and read copiously from the works of Plutarch, Montaigne and other philosophers, occasionally putting pen to paper to write an article about the boxing or athletics scene of the day.

When not doing this, he would take walks to the brow of the nearby land, where he would have had a panoramic view of the Clyde basin below, shrouded for the most part in the mist and foggy smoke of the vast heavy engineering and shipbuilding on the banks of the river. He would have seen ship number 534 laid down at the John Brown yard in 1930 and steadily grow until its launch four years later as the Cunard liner *Queen Mary*, which in 1936 would, on its maiden voyage, capture the Blue Riband for the fastest Atlantic crossing by returning from New York in under four days.

He was also a bit of a professional punter and tipster, making occasional forays into the city to visit bookmakers.

He had managed one moment of reflected glory – having been presented with Tommy's Military Cross by King George V in a ceremony at Ibrox Park football stadium.

Meanwhile Nancy (and Billy, now called Jack) entered a post-war world where there was a massive gender imbalance.

Her adopting uncle John Black died in 1919, and Nancy and Billy shared their time between Carlisle and Wilmslow. Abersoch in North Wales was a popular holiday destination for the Lee family on account of its sailing, and while there Nancy met and became friendly with a Cheshire stockbroker called Fred Tattersall. Fred was the third of four sons of John Lincoln Tattersall*, a Manchester cotton trader and mill owner who was also briefly the Liberal Member of Parliament for Stalybridge. Fred had joined up in 1915, serving with the 6th Battalion Manchester Regiment at the Somme and then in Flanders, where he was gassed in 1917, and also suffered a painful injury when he jumped into a trench and fell on a comrade's bayonet.

The friendship between Nancy and Fred developed and they got married in Carlisle on 26 April 1924 – exactly a year after the future King George the Sixth married Elizabeth Bowes Lyon. They settled in Timperley in Cheshire, where Nancy had two more sons, Ralph born in 1927 and Robin three years later. Fred left the Stock Exchange after the 1929 crash and went into partnership with his younger brother Frank, running a garage.

Ralph Erskine's widow Lennie also remarried. Her second husband was Douglas Lyall Grant, an extrovert widower who had spent two years in a German prisoner-of-war camp and whose first wife had tragically died in 1921 while giving birth to their second child, Daphne. He already had a son Colin, and he and Lennie went on to have two daughters, Jane and Susan, bringing the family to five in total. Douglas was a pillar of the London Scottish community, becoming President of both the

---

*John Tattersall's father, Cornelius Tattersall, was also a cotton merchant, and president of the Manchester Cotton Exchange. During the American Civil War, he was instrumental in sourcing cotton from Egypt, thus reducing the Union's dependence on cotton from the Confederacy. Family legend has it that after the war was over, US President Ulysses S Grant used to send him a box of cigars every Christmas as a thank you.

London Caledonian Society and London Scottish rugby club. He was a noted bon viveur, and his conviviality is still spoken of in hushed tones in the Richmond clubhouse.

So my father acquired a step-father when he was seven and then two much younger half- brothers. He was sent to a prep school called St Chad's in Prestatyn in North Wales and then went to Brighton College.

When he left school, he bought himself a car – an old Morgan, I think – with a view to driving it home to Cheshire. (At that time there were no driving tests.) This was a two-day journey in those days and on day one he broke down while driving round Marble Arch, whereupon a taxi driver shouted at him 'put a penny in the meter mate'. In the evening he stopped for the night and parked in a field. It was a chilly evening but he had to give priority to putting his coat over the engine so that it would start the next day, while he shivered on the back seat. When he finally arrived home in triumph after a journey of about 36 hours, Fred enquired how much he'd paid for the car. 'Five pounds,' said Dad proudly. 'Four pounds ten shillings too bloody much,' retorted Fred.

In December of the same year he recalled being at a 21st birthday party at the Midland Hotel in Manchester at which the festivities were paused so that the guests could crowd round a radio in the corner of the ballroom to hear King Edward the Eighth abdicate from the throne to which he had recently succeeded.

Although a bright pupil, he chose not to go on to university. He joined ICI as a laboratory assistant at Blackley in North Manchester in May 1935, and was commissioned into the Territorial Army in the same year. He attended several annual army camps and also took a holiday in Hitler's Germany in 1936. He played some club rugby for Manchester and briefly dated the actress Helen Cherry. But his fairly carefree lifestyle of the time came to an end in 1939 when Hitler invaded Poland and Britain went to war with Germany.

8

WORLD WAR 2 –
AND BARRIE

A s an adult, my father preferred to be known as John to those outside his family and this is how I shall refer to him to avoid confusion with his father Jack.

Having already been in the Territorial Army, John Lee was called up into the regular army on the outbreak of war, and commissioned into the Royal Army Service Corps (RASC). In April 1940 his unit went to France as part of the British Expeditionary Force. John crossed on the night of 9 April from Southampton to Cherbourg, where they unloaded their lorries and proceeded east to near Amiens.

To my everlasting regret, I never asked my father about his war experience so what follows is culled from a brief diary he kept, together with the regimental diary.

On 10 May the German offensive started and he wrote:

Early am	Bombing in St Andre & Lambersart direction
0800	Wireless news of German invasion of Low Countries

0830	Warning order from HQ – 'Stand by to move'
1100	Order from HQ 'Move at 1300 hours'
1300	Moved by road to Premesque

His unit spent the next few days near Lille but then moved into Belgium, a small village called Watou, close to Ypres, where his father had perished 23 years previously. But the German advance was virtually unchecked, until evacuation of the BEF became the only option. On return to the UK he wrote to his mother.

> As the week progressed, the situation became rapidly more untenable. Last Sunday night I had four hours very disturbed sleep (I was aroused on 3 different occasions and had to get out of bed) in a small Belgian village at the back of Ypres, having motored 30/40 miles that afternoon in 9 hours standing on the running board of the car the whole way to spot aircraft and having taken cover in ditches no less than 6 times.

These disturbed broken four hours were his last chance to sleep until Thursday evening, over 100 hours later!

His unit moved very slowly north to the coast then turned west and reached La Panne on the outskirts of Dunkirk on the Wednesday. Some of their lorries went to the beach and were driven into the water to form a makeshift pier, with troops using the half-submerged cabs as stepping stones.

At 1.30 am on 30 May the unit received written orders to throw all ammunition into the ditch, destroy any remaining lorries, and to rendezvous at Bray-Dunes, one of the beaches within the perimeter. This they did, arriving at Bray-Dunes at 6 am. They spent 16 hours there under fierce bombardment from

the Luftwaffe before boarding a ship called the *Royal Sovereign**
via the aforementioned 'Quay of Lorries' at 10 pm. Once on
board, John was able to crash out on the floor after being awake
for over four and a half days.

Nancy was staying in Abersoch while the drama of the Dunkirk
evacuation was being played out. Given that she had lost two
brothers and a husband in war, one can only begin to imagine
the anxiety she must have felt. But this will have been followed
by a wave of relief when she received a telegram sent from
Marylebone, simply saying:

Safe and sound in England Jack.

Also involved in the Dunkirk evacuation was Fred Tattersall's
brother Frank. Having served in the Tank Regiment in World
War One, Frank signed up as a naval reservist, and worked on a
pleasure steamer which had been converted to a minesweeper. His
ship was sent to assist with the evacuation but was sunk by enemy
action. Frank was fortunately rescued after spending two hours in
the water. But when, on his being returned to England, he phoned
his wife to tell her he was safe, she struggled to understand a word
he was saying. His false teeth had failed to survive the commotion
of abandoning ship, and were lying at the bottom of the Channel!

---

* *The Royal Sovereign had in civilian life carried day trippers from
Tower Pier to Calais and Boulogne and weekend trippers to Ostend – a
trip which could then be made on a 'no passport' basis for just over £2
including a night's accommodation. In autumn 1939, she was involved in
the evacuation of children and expectant mothers from Dagenham and
Gravesend to Great Yarmouth then was briefly a troop transport ship
operating between Southampton and Cherbourg. She undertook nine trips
to/from Dunkirk, rescuing 16,000 troops, before her brief but eventful
career came to a sad end on 9 December 1940, when she was mined and
sunk in the Bristol Channel.*

The 'miracle of Dunkirk' succeeded in getting over 300,000 of the BEF home, though most of their equipment had been destroyed or abandoned. The fall of France followed, and the summer of 1940 saw the maximum danger until the RAF defied the Luftwaffe in the Battle of Britain. In early September, when an invasion was still a strong possibility, John Lee was on leave in Abersoch and went to a dance. A girl took his fancy so he asked her to dance, saying 'Please may I have the next dance? In fact please may I have every other dance for the rest of the evening?' The girl in question was Zoe Nicoll, an actress and the youngest of four daughters of Jim Nicoll, a Scottish couturier who owned a fashionable dress shop in Luton. John never relinquished his prey and after a whirlwind courtship they got engaged and were married in Harpenden on 26 April 1941 – Nancy and Fred's 17th anniversary.

The best man at the wedding was Barrie Erskine, Ralph and Lennie's son and John's cousin and best friend. Barrie had grown up in Wimbledon with his four half-siblings. He went to school at Harrow and acquired a reputation for his wit and good company. Before the war, he dated a lady with the splendid name of Ferelith Kenworthy (who went on to marry a baronet!).

Writing in a book about the last 'deb season' before the war, called *1939: The Last Season of Peace*, she described being embarrassed by Barrie at the annual Eton v Harrow cricket match at Lord's.

> He was an Old Harrovian, and at the end of the match he disappeared onto the pitch to join the general scrum which ensued, with top hats, straw boaters and umbrellas flying everywhere through the air. Imagine my dismay, as an eighteen-year-old, at being thus deserted by my young male escort!

When war broke, out Barrie joined the Argyll and Sutherland Highlanders. He had also been courting Zoe and she had to make a choice between the two cousins. Barrie was in Scotland when Zoe sent him a telegram to say she and John were engaged. He replied with characteristic good grace while in quite a spiritual mood.

10.30 pm 29.1.41

Your wire made my birthday perfect, thank you Zoe. I have not written sooner because as you know one must have time and mood. Many a time my head has said 'You must write. It's rude'. But heart has said 'To Hell! Oi'll write when oi want to.'

Your letter arrived too on the same day. I won't comment because we don't write that sort of letter. At least I'm trying hard to get out of it. Just one thing, I did get your letter about dreams for sale. Oh, and just one more. I was glad to see that after eight (very beautiful) pages of keeping to the lines you went all skew-whiff on the last two.

Now to tell you how this famous mood and opportunity has occurred.

I have been sent with six men to look after a lot of our stuff on a 7,500 ton boat in the middle of the Firth of Clyde. The ship is manned by Poles who, like all of their race, are charming fellows. My responsibilities are nil, my work nil. I have absolutely nothing to do.

You can have no idea how I enjoy it. I have brought many books and read to my heart's content, then I muse and chew my pipe and then I write a bit and so it goes on. No one ever bothers me and I only speak to the Officers at meal times. It is the best thing that has happened to me since my week's leave. I am learning poetry by heart too, I recite to the seagulls on the boat deck. It is freedom.

I have just come in from a short walk on deck. I stopped and leant over the rail. It is a pitch black night with heavy cloud and a strong wind. No human sound, only the sea surging past the boat. No mastheads save those of the slumbering tramp steamers anchored in the estuary. It was so dark I couldn't see the sea beneath me nor the sky above. I was unaware of my body even, and the wind chased past me. I was just me, a spirit void of a physical feeling floating in the air.

I felt as I have so often wanted to be, free of all mundane ties, at liberty to wander without my body.

As ever I had to come and write of it to you. It may not sound much in my limp words; in fact or I should say, in dream, it was very deep. I know you understand.

I am going to bed now. I will read from the Spirit of Man.

Goodnight. B

A few days later he also wrote to his aunt Nancy.

19 Augramont Rd, Hamilton   5.2.41

Dearest Auntie Nancy,

Thank you for your kind letter.

I came back from a week aboard ship in the Clyde to find letters from Jack, Zoe and yourself waiting for me.

I cannot tell you how deeply happy I feel about the whole thing.

I must admit that on reading the news I felt a mild stab in the entrails but this was followed by such a rush of happiness that I did not quite know what to do with myself. It is indeed a happy match, just as their courting has been in this lovely Welsh country instead of suburbia, so I do think their marriage will be finer and nobler than anything originating from the town.

I have wired and written Jack warning him that I shall make every effort to assist the consumption of any ale which may be provided at his nuptials.

I have also written Zoe of my willingness to become an uncle when I am called upon to be so.

I wish I were with you now. There must be some great form in Abersoch.

All my love dear Auntie Nancy

Barrie

PS I have learnt the first two parts of The Ancient Mariner by heart (35 verses). I am liable to recite them at any moment.

The relatively gentle life in Scotland did not last and by 1943 Barrie's 8th Battalion was sent to Tunisia as part of the allied action to expel Rommel's Axis forces from Africa. Before departure he had leave which he spent at Abersoch, where Ralph Tattersall remembers his standing with his back to the fire and causing mild shock by lifting his regimental kilt to warm his backside.

From Tunisia he wrote to my parents, while on a couple of rest days in a hotel:

1 February 1943

Last night for the first time since I came out here, I slept in a proper bed with sheets. I also had my first proper bath. Three of us arrived from my battalion with four bottles of whisky and four of gin, we were taking no chances. Funnily enough the place is called Ain Dramm! Most appropriate. There are also civilians here among whom is a Jew, the 'Woolworth King' of Tunisia, who has a wife and a mistress who all appear to share the same room. Whether or not they actually sleep in the same triple bed, I do not know.

Continuing two days later:

The sun has just gone down behind a scrub-covered hill, it is getting chilly. A few moments ago, twelve Stukas came over, black against the sky.They dived almost perpendicularly, down, down, the ack-ack opened up all around and they flattened out and turned away, pink in the setting sun, with the gentle cotton-wool puffs of smoke forming around them. They were some distance away and all I could hear was the vroom of their engines. The whole affair was quite lovely, for all the world they might have been moths playing in the firelight. Strange. All that is left now are the widening wisps in the evening air.

We have had a cloudless day and now the sun is setting, a few transparent courtiers have come to pay him their respects before he goes to bed. Some are black, some are blood red, and some are orange. Across the sky from the sun, the night is feeling its purple way upwards.

Two months later, a long letter to my mother Zoe gives an evocative description of rural North Africa at that time.

4 April 1943

My dear Zoe,
    I was most happy to get your last letter. I love your letters above all from the others I get, you write just as

you are, and so I can read and re-read them with more and more appreciation. Today I went for one of my rare baths and had with it a complete change. Like the absent-minded idiot I am, I left your letter in the pocket of my old battle-dress. It is now probably being churned round in some cleaning machine while I am left to mourn its loss.

Much has happened since I last wrote. As I think I told you Charles Cole my great friend of London days is missing and as if that was not enough six of my greatest friends here have all been wounded leaving me very much alone. I must thank my lucky stars for my own escape as last week when all this occurred I was away from the battalion acting as liaison officer with the French. My two particular friends were very lucky to come off so lightly. The battalion order group was getting its orders from the C.O. (I would inevitably have been there) when they were machine gunned by a Messerschmitt, which got them at the third attempt. Tommy was wounded in the side and James, whose haversack was ripped off him, got one through the arm.

I myself had one narrow shave on the same road when attacked by a Messerschmitt. I saw it coming, hopped off my motor-bike, ran up the bank and as luck would have it found a weapon pit and jumped in. Over he came with his guns rattling and dropped a bomb. It had a delayed fuse and went off with a bang just as I poked my head out of the hole. My left ear drum nearly burst and I could scarcely get out of my lair for the earth on top of me. I paced the distance from my shelter to the crater – it was ten yards.

The countryside is more perfect than ever. Today on my drive over to the baths the colours on the hillside made a most vivid impression on my European eyes. Bright emerald green fields thinning into unimaginable shades of brown and red against the soil which is in parts crimson. Stretches of pure orange where marigolds were thicker than clover, other fields clear yellow and some a more vivid magenta than any countess's evening frock. Sharp sided wadis wriggled through the fields, changing into strong ravines as they reached the mountains. The mountains themselves were not to be outdone – some were crimson and on others outcrops of delicate pink glistened in the sun, but their shapes were best of all. Sculptured by the hammer and chisel of wind and rain wielded by the heavy hand of time they were pure fantasy. Here lions crouched, there a dragon or an army advanced in proud display along a skyline, trumpets blowing towards the battlements of an enchanted castle whose turrets, keep and loop-holed walls glowered down from inaccessible heights.

But I enthuse – to turn from nature to the hand of man.

Two days ago I visited a city of the dead – a Roman city in a remarkable state of preservation from where the high road ran straight to ancient Carthage.

I was led round by an old and lecherous Arab who slunk along in a pair of British army socks and plimsolls over the massive stones of roman streets. Firstly the amphitheatre, where I imagine toga'd citizens sitting row on row on the granite seats while the players proclaimed from the stage below and I just thought how in 50 AD any good Roman who was tired with the play could gaze at the lovely Tunisian landscape as I had done. Thence on to a temple with its graceful Corinthian columns decorating the sky. Here I saw inscriptions carved in stone with a touch so fine and a spacing so precise as to make amateurs out of our modern-day carvings. Here and there a headless statue added his vacancy to the roofless temple. The door was twenty feet high with door posts two foot square of one flawless stone on which was set the massive lintel. All weighing many tons each and brought from a quarry five miles away.

Then to the forum carpeted with green grass. On from house to house with their delicate mosaic floors, beautifully proportioned doorways the threshold still scraped by an ill-fitting door. The deep ingrained arcs an eternal witness to a clumsy Roman carpenter.

Then a twinkle came into my cicerone's* eye. 'This was a brothel' said he indicating to me a phallic sign carved on a stone outside. A spacious court where fountains played and round it a pillared cloister off which gave little intimate rooms where the Romans might enjoy the pleasures of the house. And, sanitary people that they were, you might have a bath too.

Next came, from my Arab's point of view, the piece de resistance – the public lavatory, which he called by its British Army name, having learnt it no doubt from the inevitable ejaculation of a hundred soldiers on seeing this monument to Roman sanitation.

There were twelve neat holes cut in a semi-circular stone plinth. Not unlike a type of garden seat on the terraces of English country houses. Just in case the physical application of the lavabo had not been fully grasped, my guide leapt neatly in a crouching position on one of the holes and began to make appropriate noises.

At last I paid him off in an olive grove littered with broken columns and moss covered stones. I sat down

---

*An old-fashioned word for a guide

to muse over this strange city set on a hill and now fighting off the clustering Arab huts around it who had taken its stones but not its grandeur.

Suddenly I became aware of a distant chanting. Thinking it might be some religious ceremony, I went to have a look. It took a long time pottering through the ruins before I tracked the wailing down. At the corner of a courtyard I saw a door, piled in the threshold was a heap of tiny shoes with one big pair balanced on top. It was bright sunlight outside so it wasn't till I was very near I could see inside – an Arab school. Seated on the floor of a small room were twenty to thirty little cross-legged Arab boys each with a little red cap on his head and each clasping a board in his hands on which was written a verse of the Koran, as far as I could see a different verse for each one. All were chanting their verses as loud as they could. In the centre sat the imam, an old and wizened Arab in the traditional white robe. He commented on the wailing of his pupils by an occasional Ah! Ah! and when that failed or if one particular boy offended he would whack at him or his lesson board with a long stick which he held in his hand and with which he could reach to the farthermost corner of the room.

When I arrived the wailing fell like a run-down gramophone and when I executed a few lumbering pas or basques in the doorway complete silence reigned and the pupils giggled impishly at one another. No amount of ah ahing could avert the wail. The Imam had to resort to his flail, the blows fell thick and fast on pupil and board alike. Till gathering strength the requisite din was attained.

I crept away leaving the teacher and his class as they
had been for the last one thousand years.
All love to you and Jack if he is back.
Barrie

Tragically, less than three weeks later Barrie too was dead. His
battalion was involved in the Battle of Longstop Hill, which took
place from 21 to 23 April 1943. The battle was fought for control
over the heights of Djebel al Ahmera and Djebel Rhar, together
known as Longstop Hill and vicinity, between the British forces
of the First Army under Montgomery and German units of the
5th Panzer Army under Rommel.

This (edited) description is taken from Wikipedia.

At 11:30 am the Surreys and the Argylls advanced
but German machine guns and mortars began to
inflict casualties on the start line, which made it
impossible for the Argylls to capture the main hills
during the hours of darkness, so another plan was
made to seize the Djebel Ahmera (the western half
of Longstop).

The Argylls were supported along the southern
slopes of Longstop by two squadrons of the North
Irish Horse. Behind heavy concentrations of artillery,
the Highlanders went up the Djebel Ahmera ridge
through heavy machine-gun fire, advancing in box
formation through a cornfield. As they reached the
base of the hill, the commanding officer was killed
by shellfire and the attack soon lost cohesion but
Major 'Jock' Anderson soon took over command
and urged the Argylls to press on. Despite heavy
casualties, the Argylls climbed up the hill and were
soon among the defenders and started to eliminate

the ring of machine-gun nests. For inspiring his men and eliminating strong points during the fighting around Djebel Ahmera, Anderson was later awarded the Victoria Cross. His battalion had been reduced to 44 officers and men.

By nightfall, the Argylls, reinforced by the Surreys, had managed to complete the capture of Djebel Ahmera along with 200 prisoners and held the hill.

Another eye-witness account said:

After several false starts the barrage etc went at 1130 and the Argylls followed onto Longstop Hill with pipes playing. David Brown (Forward Observation Officer) was killed. He and Paul lost two killed and three wounded plus three missing in their OP parties. It's stupid to put valuable technicians in front where they are away from their communications and useless. A hairy day for the infantry.

Barrie was one of those in front – he was laying a telephone line when he was killed. The victory at Longstop Hill was a key point in the advance to Tunis, which finally eliminated the German and Italian presence in Africa.

Barrie's death meant that Nancy was now James Erskine's only descendant. Despite his having had five children, nobody now remains in his branch of the family with the Erskine name. My mother told me that my father never really recovered from losing his cousin and soulmate.

On 4 August 1944 Ralph's great friend and subsequently brother-in-law Charles Higgins wrote:

The thirtieth anniversary of the First German War – or
is it the same war as this, which never really ended?

At that time Ralph Erskine and I rushed down from
Arran, and quite without any notion of wisdom, walked
out on a tight-rope of fate. Ralph was an Olympic
runner and world champion feather-weight boxer. He
was nearly across when something went wrong – and I
think he had no parachute. Now his son Barrie, adorable
as his father and as charming to look at, has gone down
in Africa.

There was about these two a kind of brightness
that should be spoken of, though it is impossible to
describe. The father was at all times ready to receive
and delight, while there was about the son a sort of
diffidence that is found in a few of the beautiful and
foredoomed – almost as though they were apologising
for being what they are, and for troubling awhile with
their presence those more firmly tied to earth.

Back in the UK, my parents spent their first years together
in married quarters at various army training camps such as
Ampleforth, Scarborough, and Catterick , preparing for the
invasion of Europe – an event which almost coincided with the
birth of their first child – me! My mother returned to her parents'
house in Harpenden and I arrived – a month prematurely, I
believe – on 21 June 1944, a couple of weeks after D-day.

My father wasn't around to enjoy fatherhood first hand for
long as his 388 Company RASC crossed to France in August
1944, arriving in Cherbourg just over four years after he had left
Dunkirk. From there he headed east following the allied advance
until he reached Brussels, which had just been liberated. He
remained there until he was demobbed, and was awarded the
MBE for the efficiency with which he organised the transport.

The war had one final victim from the family. Ralph Erskine's half-brother Colin Lyall Grant, a lieutenant in the Royal Indian Army Service Corps, was killed in Burma in August 1944 aged 29.

9

AFTER WORLD WAR 2

My father was demobbed in March 1946 with the rank of lieutenant-colonel and returned to his pre-war career at ICI. After a short refresher course, he was given a sales job in London. We lived in Muswell Hill, a house in Ringwood Avenue I can just remember, before he was transferred back to Manchester in 1948 as I described in the introduction.

Fred and Nancy Tattersall were now living in Didsbury. Ralph Tattersall went to school at Gordonstoun, and then spent time as a cadet on the training ship HMS *Conway* in North Wales, before joining the Merchant Navy as a junior officer with the Blue Star Line. Robin was at Manchester Grammar School, where he played rugby for the first fifteen. He then did national service, being sent to Trieste, which was then an iron-curtain flashpoint being claimed by both Italy and Yugoslavia.

Ralph first met Granddaddy in 1945, travelling north to join his first ship. He recalls:

He met me at the bottom of the track that leads up from the Rutherglen to East Kilbride road, past the

Italian prisoner-of-war camp, where he befriended several of the prisoners whilst they were out on day release at nearby farms during the last war. We had a wonderful evening together, bearing in mind I had never met him before nor been north of the border for that matter, and I left hoping to see him again.

It was almost two years before I returned to Glasgow having left the Merchant Navy, and was on my way to Elgin to renew acquaintance with a girlfriend, calling off to see him en route. It was the winter of 1947/8 and the snow lay thick on the ground. The following morning before breakfast he took me outside where, stripping naked, we had a snow bath amongst the bracken. After that we did some physical exercises. He was still very strong and, after my poor efforts to 'put the weight', proceeded to throw the heavy cannon ball about ten feet further than myself.

On this visit he also took me to see the famous Rangers v Celtic football match at Ibrox Stadium. We were Rangers supporters standing on the Celtic terraces – something which would probably have got us lynched nowadays.

Granddaddy continued to live his solitary existence but as he was now over 80, this way of life was a worry to Nancy. In 1948 he had a dispute with a neighbouring farmer over trespass rights and was attacked with a pitchfork (!) resulting in his receiving two broken arms. This persuaded him that it was no longer a good idea to continue to live on his own and he agreed to come south and live with Fred and Nancy in Didsbury. Which is how I came to play dominoes with him.

Ralph's recollection again:

> His subsequent move south to live with us brought a great deal of pleasure to my brother Robin and me, and his influence was felt by the whole family. His encouragement in all things to do with our physical and mental development was welcomed, and could hardly go unnoticed by others. His stentorian blandishments would echo across the nearby Southern Cemetery playing fields as we were induced to better and better performances. His efforts were particularly rewarded by my younger brother, who was a much more promising pupil.
>
> Whilst my father (Fred) and Granddaddy got on well, they used to have the most heated arguments about politics. My father, who was not particularly partisan but paid lip service to the Conservative Party, used to bait Granddaddy mercilessly about the changes taking place in the post-war Attlee government – the National Health Service, Nationalisation, etc – knowing full well that Granddaddy was passionately committed to the cause and furtherance of socialism.
>
> They also had a harmonising common interest in loving to bet on horse racing. I don't suppose they did any better than other punters. Granddaddy was, I think, a suppressed gambler but fortunately neither of them took it too seriously. His other pleasures were the *Guardian* crossword and Alastair Cooke's *Letter from America*.
>
> He would join us for holidays at Abersoch and on several occasions could be found crewing for my father in his boat along with Monty, our Gordon setter.

Robin Tattersall recalls:

> I do remember him putting me to shame because his chest expansion was so much bigger than mine. He tried to make a track and field athlete out of me and we would go out onto the big field opposite our house in Manor Drive to train.
>
> One summer when we were all down in Abersoch, I took part in a running race at the Village Sports. When I got home, Granddaddy asked me how I had done and when I replied that I had come last but the winner had won half a crown, Granddaddy paled and said to me in horror 'Now you've done it. You will never be able to take part in the Olympics because you have taken part in a race for money'.

In the autumn of 1951 while on a nocturnal visit to the toilet, he had a heavy fall which shook him up to the point of pneumonia. He was taken to Davyhulme Hospital and after a week or two was cured of this by the medics. But, in Ralph's words, 'he just turned his face to the wall and let life slip away'. He died in October 1951, two days after his 86th birthday.

The following spring, Ralph rode his motorbike up to Scotland and scattered Granddaddy's ashes over the brae where he had lived alone for almost thirty years.

POST SCRIPT

Granddaddy's death spared him from enduring one final tragedy. The following September Nancy became yet another member of the Erskine family to meet an untimely death.

She was a keen golfer but had never learned to drive a car, so used to cycle everywhere. While returning from a game at Northenden Golf Club, her wheel was clipped by a motorbike while she was crossing the busy Princess Parkway, and she was thrown into the road. This was a busy road even then – now it's part of the M56! She was also deaf in one ear from a childhood illness, which may have been a contributory factor, and safety helmets were then a thing of the future.

She was admitted to Withington Hospital with a suspected fractured skull and detained overnight. Fred visited her in the evening and left at 11 pm. She had not only sustained a fractured skull, but also internal bleeding (which would probably have been detected had it happened today). This led to a fatal cerebral haemorrhage and she died at 1 am, less than two weeks after her 55th birthday.

I was eight at the time and can just remember the terrible sense of shock for my dad, who had already lost his father, and of course to Ralph and Robin.

I tried a few years ago to get a copy of the inquest report but those from that year had recently been thrown away. My mother told me that the motorcyclist was fined £10 for driving without due care and attention.

Her sons Ralph and Robin both married shortly after their mother's death, and Fred remarried a few years later, going on to have two more children. He died in 1975 aged 78.

Ralph loved his time at sea, and was thrilled at a young age to sail the seas and see the world. Unfortunately, after a short time at sea, personal circumstances led to him leaving the Merchant Navy. However, his natural charm and charisma meant that he was not long out of employment and he made a successful career in sales. Ralph continued his love of the sea. He has spent many hours on the water in North Wales and is a founding member of Holyhead Sailing Club. He is a talented artist, a realistic clay bust of Granddaddy being a particularly noteworthy creation.

Robin had gone to university at Cambridge after his national service and subsequently, in addition to playing top-level rugby for London Scottish, qualified as a surgeon. In 1965 he took the bold step of going out to the Caribbean as the British government surgeon to the British Virgin Islands. After two tours of duty he remained in the BVI, where he set up and ran a very successful private clinic, and was awarded an OBE for services to the community. He represented the BVI at sailing in the 1984 Los Angeles Olympics. This involved swearing an affidavit to say he was a true amateur, and for a couple of days before he signed, Robin says he was haunted by a vision of Granddaddy up above shaking his head! Robin's involvement with the Olympic movement didn't end there – he was official doctor to the BVI team at the London Olympics in 2012, and marched with the team in Danny Boyle's memorable opening ceremony.

Ralph and Robin each had four children so including my sister Rosalind and myself, there are 10 great-grandchildren, who between them have, to date, produced 16 great-great-grandchildren, and 5 great-great-great-grandchildren. So, including his grandchildren Ralph and Robin, Granddaddy has a total of 33 living descendants.

But sadly, none of them bears the Erskine surname.

Robert Lee 2020

APPENDIX A

O n 2 April 1915, this description based on Tommy's diaries was published in *The Glasgow Herald*. Place names had been removed by the censors.

A GORDON OFFICER'S DIARY

LIVELINESS IN THE TRENCHES

The following extracts from the diary of a young officer attached to the Gordons indicate that, even when there is officially 'nothing to report', life in the field is by no means uneventful or unexciting. The writer was one of the first members of the Glasgow University Officers' Training Corps to be appointed to a commission, and he has been at the front since the middle of December. He is a member of a family prominent in Scottish amateur boxing and athletics circles, and prior to the war was Hon. Secretary to one of our oldest cross-country clubs.

'I've had a fairly strenuous time this tour. After two days in reserve trench our C.O. sent me with two men to occupy a trench which had been dug by sappers in the dark. We were to ascertain by daylight whether it was enfiladed by German trenches. I had been up at the firing line from midnight to 2 am with a working party. Having slept on the straw in the farm kitchen for a couple of hours, I was up again at 4 am and trekking away to get to the new trench before daylight. Fortunately for us it was not enfiladed, and so having found the only comparatively dry portion of it we made ourselves as comfortable as we could. My shoulders were hard up against the sides, and as it was difficult to turn around we did not bother cooking a meal, but at midday we had a repast of cold bully-beef and bread. I had an apple in my pocket and shared it with my men for dessert. At dusk – about 6.30 pm – we left the trench and went back to the farm.

I forgot to mention a rather exciting time we had late on Sunday afternoon before we left the reserve farm. Suddenly at about 4.30 pm just as we (the officers) were at tea in the kitchen, there was a sound as of a storm rising – a whizzing as of a strong wind. In a moment the shells were bursting all round the farmhouse. In another second all our guns were answering, and there ensued a most terrific artillery duel. Our company was immediately ordered out of the barns and into the dug-outs. We heard rapid firing up at the trenches and thought that the Germans must be delivering an attack. We were ordered to hold ourselves ready to go at dusk if the bombardment should continue, and take up our positions in the second line of trenches. The tremendous cannonade was kept up for an hour and a quarter, and by some miracle we did not have a single casualty, although the roofs were being brought down from the buildings and barns beside us and the shells were bursting everywhere around us. All our guns behind were going full pelt and ultimately, having established a superiority of fire of at least three to one, they silenced the German guns altogether, and we went back to finish our tea. We learned next morning that the Germans had taken some of our trenches at ____. Their aim had been to keep us on the defensive and prevent us from sending along supplies. We retook all the trenches except two small portions the next night. There had been no infantry attack on our trenches.

GRENADING

I had a rather tricky job on hand last night. With two of my men (old soldiers who have both been out since the beginning) I crawled out over 100 yards in front of our barbed wire. We lay flat and I sent five rifle grenades into the German trenches. Each time I fired I drew the rifle fire and flares of the enemy. Several flares landed just beside us, and showed us up very plainly to our people behind – but of course they knew where to look for us. When the flares were up we lay flat as if dead, and the Germans failed to spot us, being unable to distinguish us from the dead men lying all around us (I was lying beside a dead German). We watched the flash of the rifle of a sniper about 150 yards in front, and I put the grenades in his direction. I hope I got someone in the trench. I think I did, as my grenades all went off well, and just where I aimed them. We lay out for an hour and a half watching and listening for a German patrol, but no advance parties came forward. In going back to our lines we landed in trenches 100 yards from our own (it is so easy to lose one's direction when crawling in the dark). Luckily for us, the other trenches had been warned we were out, or we might have been shot for Germans.

We had as a battalion to do an extra day on duty on account of the thinning of the line by the recent fighting at ____. Our company therefore when relieved from the trenches last night came back into the support farm instead of going to ____. The extra day on duty proved a disastrous one for us. We have had no casualties at the farm since Gordon was wounded here two months ago. Today, however, the Germans shelled us with shrapnel very heavily. A shell came right through the door of one of the barns, killing five men instantly and wounding another eleven. We have had a terrible time bandaging the wounded. The tragedy occurred at two o'clock, and they had to lie waiting all afternoon for dusk, when they were carried back to the dressing station. The dead men are being buried out behind the farm. Three of them were in a shocking condition. I saw them in the barn. Their heads had all been blown off, leaving the trunks mangled and the flesh and blood splattered against the walls. It was a dreadful sight. As usual, too, some of the few remaining old hands suffered – two out of the five killed came out with the battalion, and had been through thick and thin with it. Another had just returned with the last draft, having been home wounded. The terrible feature of thus being shelled in buildings is that one doesn't have any chance of retaliating – we don't know which guns behind the hill are getting us – we simply wait in suspense till it's all over, and it's just a toss-up whether we escape or not. We had been congratulating ourselves on having had no casualties in the firing line in our company and then – 16 in one fell swoop. And we really should not have been here at all, but back at ____. Such are the fortunes of war! We have supped on horrors today: but it is impossible not to admire the bearing of the wounded men, some of them very seriously, *and perhaps fatally, hurt who are* lying *patiently suffering behind the farm, waiting for the stretcher-bearers.*

WAR A HELLISH BUSINESS

One of the poor fellows today had been set on fire by the shell, and the ammunition in his pouches was exploding in the barn. A pail of water had to be thrown over him to extinguish the flames, and his body was all charred when I saw him. Ugh! War is a hellish business. The sergeant-major has just come in to tell me that one of the wounded men died before they arrived at the dressing station. Well that's six dead so far. Not a bad toll for one small shell.

We had a fire in our billets here today, the main barn, in which three-quarters of our company lodged, being burned to the ground. If we come back to _____ (which is doubtful) we shall have to find a new farm.

We are now in a support farm. There is no kitchen and we (the officers) are occupying pens in a stable – just like a lot of cattle. We can't have any coke fires during daylight, as the slightest vestige of smoke escaping outside would at once be spotted by the hawks' eyes of the enemy's observers, and we would be showered with shells. However, by dint of careful stoking we (there are four of us) managed to boil two canteens of water on a small fire made in a bully-beef tin and composed of small shavings of wood, so as to make no smoke. We had a good breakfast of tea, tinned veal, and boiled eggs. We won't get any more food cooked till after dark (about 8 pm at the earliest).

Our new trenches are much nearer the Germans than our last ones were. Indeed my section, which is the most forward, is only about 40 yards from them. Their trench is just on the outside of a small wood and mine less than a stone's throw across. We have to be very careful. All look-outs by day use periscopes and the latter must not be exposed for more than a few seconds at a time, or they will be spotted and shot at. My periscope was shot twice, each time right through the thin wooden stem. The French occupied this position for a long time, and seem to have made several unsuccessful attempts at further advance, as their dead are scattered all over the place. To my right is a regular row of about 25 corpses about 5 yards in front of our trench. The French evidently tried to advance in line from this trench and had a machine gun turned on them, mowing them down in a line.

We went back to the support farm on Sunday night, and returned to the firing line last (Tuesday) night, so that of the last ten days we have spent only two in billets. There is no prospect of a relief yet. We go back to the reserve farm tomorrow night, and after two days there we will return to the firing line unless the battalion is relieved. I hope we'll get a longer spell in billets when the relief does come. The men are ready for a rest now and they have well earned it. The Germans yesterday put a rifle grenade into the trench on our right, killing one officer and wounding six men of the Suffolks. I hope my grenades have accounted for a good many of the enemy.

After a long spell of dry weather we have had two wet days. The trench is in a frightfully mucky state. M'Callum evacuated this dugout last night and left our old friend Neil Lyon's 'Arthur' and 'The Isle of Unrest' by Henry Seton Merriman for me to read. I had breakfast about 8 am – bacon and eggs. We don't light our fires till about dusk lest the smoke is seen by the enemy, so we won't have tea till about 8 pm. Though the shells are hurtling through the air incessantly, the birds are whistling in the sky above, heedless of everything except the onset of spring. How I envy them!'

APPENDIX B

THE BARRIE FAMILY

This is a contemporary record kept by Granddaddy's wife's family which illustrates their extensive involvement in the Great War.

Thomas Barrie: Sergeant 'A' Company 11th Argyll & Sutherland Highlanders. Fought at Loos 1915. Killed in France 31 May 1916 aged 25.

George Barrie: Lance Corporal 'B' Company 11th Highland Light Infantry. Middleweight champion boxer. Killed in France 31 Jan 1916 aged 21.

John Barrie: Sergeant 79th Canadian Scottish Regiment. Fought at Neuve Chapelle and 2nd Ypres (wounded & gassed). Emigrated to farm in W Australia.

James Barrie: Chemical adviser 3rd Army HQ France. Demobilised Feb 1919. Became a doctor and died at Epping in 1990 aged 93.

Robert Barrie: Trooper 10th Australian Light Horse, Holy Land. Wounded Dardanelles 1915. Survived the war then ran an orchard in New South Wales.

Alexander (Aldy) Barrie: Trooper 10th Australian Light Horse. Died in Malta of wounds received in Gallipoli 10 Oct 1915 aged 29.

Henderson Barrie: Driver 'D' Battery, RFA France. Shell shock 1916. Fought with Canadians at Vimy Ridge 1917. Emigrated to Australia in 1920, where he married. Worked as a porter and then barman in the Canberra area.

Alexander Barrie: Corporal 'C' Company 11th HLI France. Captain Kilmarnock football team 1907-10. Killed France 1 Oct 1918 aged 40.

Thomas Barrie: Lieutenant. Emigrated to Massachusetts 1910. Joined US Navy as an engineer on transport ships. Torpedoed twice by enemy submarines.

Alexander Barrie: Private. Joined 'C' Company 13th Royal Highlanders of Canada when only 17 and served in France.

 **Matador**

For exclusive discounts on Matador titles,
sign up to our occasional newsletter at
troubador.co.uk/bookshop